*Yoga Upaniṣad Series* *Volume 4*

# Yoga Kuṇḍalī Upaniṣad

## Theory and Practices for Awakening Kuṇḍalinī

Original Sanskrit text with
Transliteration, Translation and Commentary

**Commentary by**
**Swāmī Satyadharma Saraswatī**

**Translation and Transliteration by**
**Śrimukti (Ruth Perini)**

# Dedication

**To all friends, practitioners and**

**teachers of yoga,**

**and to all seekers of spiritual wisdom,**

**regardless of time or place, creed,**

**gender, age or race.**

# CONTENTS


| | | Page |
|---|---|---|
| **Introduction** | | 1 |
| **Invocation** | | 9 |
| **CHAPTER ONE** | | |
| **Verse** | | |
| **1** | Two causes of citta | 11 |
| **2-3a** | Control of prāṇa | 13 |
| **3b-4a** | Mitāhāra, moderation in diet | 15 |
| **4b-6** | Āsana, posture | 17 |
| **7-10a** | Śakticāla, raising the kuṇḍalinī | 21 |
| **10b-18** | Method of śakticāla | 25 |
| **19-21** | Kumbhaka, retention of the breath | 30 |
| **22-23** | Preparation for kumbhaka | 33 |
| **24-26a** | Sūryabheda kumbhaka | 35 |
| **26b-29** | Ujjāyī kumbhaka | 38 |
| **30-31** | Śītalī kumbhaka | 41 |
| **32-39** | Bhastrika kumbhaka | 43 |
| **40-41** | Three bandhas | 48 |
| **42-46** | Mūlabandha | 50 |
| **47-50** | Uḍḍīyana bandha | 54 |
| **51-55** | Jālandhara bandha | 57 |
| **56-58** | First obstacle to yoga | 61 |
| **59-61** | Following nine obstacles | 66 |
| **62-65** | Merging apāna and prāṇa with agni | 74 |
| **66-69a** | Awakening of kuṇḍalinī | 79 |
| **69b-73** | Falling of the nectar | 83 |
| **74-76** | Union of kuṇḍalinī with Śiva at mūlādhāra | 86 |
| **77-78** | Pranic body is the commander of all | 88 |
| **79-81** | Tearing asunder the veil of illusion | 90 |
| **82-83a** | Śakti enters brahmarandhra | 92 |
| **83b-87** | Arising of kuṇḍalinī through the granthis and cakras | 94 |

**CHAPTER TWO**


| Verse | | |
|---|---|---|
| **1-4a** | Khecarī vidyā | 99 |
| **4b-10** | Importance of khecarī | 102 |
| **11-16a** | How to acquire this knowledge | 106 |
| **16b-18a** | Khecarī bīja | 109 |
| **18b-21a** | Esoteric details of the practice | 111 |
| **21b-24a** | Benefits of the khecarī mantra | 113 |
| **24b-27** | Necessity of practice | 115 |
| **28-37a** | Method of khecarī | 117 |
| **37b-40a** | Practise slowly | 122 |
| **40b-44a** | Last stage of khecarī | 124 |
| **44b-49** | Sūtra neti, adjunct to khecarī | 127 |


**CHAPTER THREE**


| Verse | | |
|---|---|---|
| **1-2** | Auspicious days | 132 |
| **3-4a** | Renunciation | 135 |
| **4b-7a** | Manas and śakti | 137 |
| **7b-9a** | Practice of kuṇḍalinī yoga | 140 |
| **9b-13** | Stairway to enlightenment | 142 |
| **14-18a** | Significance of yoga, guru and sādhana | 144 |
| **18b-21a** | Evolution of sound and Soham | 148 |
| **21b-26** | Meditation on the ātman | 150 |
| **27-29** | Spontaneous practice of jñāna yoga | 153 |
| **30-32** | Merging with the ātman | 156 |
| **33-35** | Supreme yogi | 159 |


**Appendices**


1. Sanskrit text 162
2. Pronunciation Guide 178
3. Continuous Translation 180

**About the Author** 195
**About the Translator** 196

# Introduction

*Veda* is a Sanskrit word meaning 'knowledge'. In the context of the Vedas, it means 'revealed knowledge which is *śruti*, 'heard' from within, not taught. These ancient spiritual texts or hymns, through which we can learn much of the perceptions and insights of the early vedic seers, are grouped into four *samhitas* or collections: *Rig Veda, Yajur Veda, Sāma Veda* and *Atharva Veda*. They were revealed to enlightened beings 3,000 to 4,500 years ago or more (the Rig-Veda contains astronomical references describing occurrences in 5,000 to 3,000 BCE), and transmitted orally by the sages from generation to generation within brahmin families.

The four Vedas were considered to be divine revelations, and each word was carefully memorised. This was to ensure accurate transmission, but also because each syllable was considered to have spiritual power, its source being the supreme, eternal sound. This was a mammoth task, as there are 20,358 verses in the four Vedas, approximately two thousand printed pages. They were composed in fifteen different metres, which demanded perfect control of the breath. Georg Feuerstein describes them as 'a composite of symbol, metaphor, allegory, myth and story, as well as paradox and riddle' and their composers as 'recipients and revealers of the invisible order of the cosmos [with] inspired insights or illumined visions'1.

***Rig Veda***

The Rig Veda is the oldest spiritual text in the world and still regarded as sacred, containing 1,028 hymns or songs of 10,589 verses in praise of the divine (*rig* or *ric* meaning 'praise'). Each hymn is recognised as a *mantra*, a sacred sound vibration, which releases energy from limited material awareness, thus expanding the consciousness. It is also the earliest surviving form of Sanskrit. The illumined seers composed the hymns while established in the highest consciousness, thus able to commune with luminous beings of the higher realms. There are about 250 hymns in praise of *Indra*, the divine force behind the ocean, heavens, thunder, lightning, rain and the light of the sun; 200 of *Agni*, born of the Sun, becoming the god of sacrificial fire, and over 100 of *Soma*, who gives immortality, and who is connected to the Sun, Moon, mountains, rivers and oceans. Others are dedicated to *Varuna*, who protects cosmic order; the *Ashvins*, supreme healers; *Ushas*, goddess of the dawn; *Aditi*, goddess of eternity; and *Saraswati*, goddess of the Vedas and of music and the arts.

***Yajur Veda***

The hymns of the Yajur-Veda, Veda of Sacrifice, consist of sacrificial formulas or prayers, including those of an internal or spiritual nature, which are chanted by the *adhvaryu* (priest), who performs the sacrifice. About a third of its 1,975 verses are taken from the Rig Veda. The rest are original and in prose form.

***Sāma Veda***

The Sāma Veda, Veda of Chants, gives instructions on the chanting of vedic hymns. The majority of its 1,875 verses are from the Rig Veda; only 75 verses are original. Many of the hymns were sung by special priests during sacrificial rites. Some are still sung today.

***Atharva Veda***

The Atharva Veda, named after the seer Atharvan, whose family were great seers in vedic times, contains 731 hymns of 5,977 verses, about one fifth of which are from the RigVeda. Much of the Atharva Veda consists of magical spells and charms for gaining health, love, peace and prosperity, or taking revenge on an enemy. Possibly for this reason, the Atharva Veda was either not accepted by the orthodox priesthood, or not given the same standing as the other Vedas.

## The vedic people and their culture

The vedic people lived for over 2,500 years mainly along the banks of the Saraswati River, which was located in Northern India between the modern Ravi and Yamuna Rivers down to what is now the desert of Rajasthan. The Saraswati River dried up in about 1,900 BCE due to tectonic upheavals. Other areas of habitation included the Ganges River and its tributaries, rivers in Afghanistan (previously called Gandhara), the Himalayas and Mount Kailash in Tibet.

The vedic people had a complex multi-tiered view of the universe, in which humankind, nature and the divine are intertwined and interrelated. They had a deep knowledge of the oceans, mountains, deserts and forests of the physical world, as well as of the subtle worlds of deities and different levels of consciousness. People lived in cities or villages or were nomads, and were fully engaged in worldly life. They were an agrarian people, yet also had herds of cattle, horses and camels. Cities were constructed of stone, bricks and metal. They built chariots and ships. They were skilled workers in gold, metal, clay, stone, wood, leather and wool, and showed a very high standard in arts, crafts, astrology, medicine, music, dance and poetry.

## After the Vedas

The Vedas were the foundation for the later revelations (*śruti*) in the *Brāhmaṇas* (ritual texts), the *Āranyakas* (texts on rituals and meditation for forest-dwelling ascetics) and the *Upaniṣads* (esoteric texts). Later still, the Vedas were the basis for numerous works of remembered or traditional knowledge, known as *smṛti,* including the epics: i.e. the *Mahābhārata, Rāmāyaṇa* and *Purāṇas,* and the *Sūtras,* or threads of knowledge, e.g. *Yoga Sūtras.* All these texts contain many concepts and practices, which come directly from the four Vedas.

## Upaniṣads

The word *upaniṣad* is comprised of three roots: *upa* or 'near', *ni* or 'attentively', and *sad,* 'to sit'. The term describes the situation in which these unique texts were transmitted. The students or disciples sat near the realized master and listened attentively, as he expounded his experiences and understanding of the ultimate reality. These teachings are said to destroy the ignorance or illusion of the spiritual aspirant in regard to what is self and non-self, what is real and unreal, in relation to the absolute and relative reality. Only disciples were chosen, who had persevered in *sādhana catuṣṭaya,* the four kinds of spiritual effort, viz. *viveka* (discrimination between the permanent and impermanent), *vairagya* (non-attachment), *ṣadsampatti* ( six virtues of serenity, self-control, withdrawal of the senses, endurance, perfect concentration and strong faith) and *mumukṣutva* (intense desire for liberation).

The Upaniṣads are derived from the Āranyakas, because they were chanted in the forest (*āranya*) after the aspirant had retired from worldly life. They are recorded in the later form of Sanskrit used in the Brāhmaṇas, and considered the last phase of *śruti*, vedic revelation. The Upaniṣads are regarded as *vedānta*, the end of the Vedas, inferring that *vedānta* is the end or completion of all perceivable knowledge, as they guide the aspirant beyond the limited mind to the *ātman* (spiritual self) and thus to *mokṣa* (liberation). Each upaniṣad reflected the teachings and tradition of a realized master, and was connected with a specific Veda and vedic school. It is estimated that there are over 200 Upaniṣads, which have been divided into seven groups: *Major*, *Vedānta*, *Śaiva, Śakta, Vaiśnava, Sannyasa* and *Yoga*.

## Yoga Upaniṣads

The twenty one Yoga Upaniṣads give an understanding of the hidden forces in nature and human beings, and describe esoteric yogic practices by which these forces can be manipulated and controlled. They emphasise that the inner journey to the one permanent reality, the *ātman*, is the essential one. Journeys to external places, such as holy sites and temples, as well as rituals and ceremonies, are not given importance. Their teachings give important information on the subtle body (*cakras, koṣas, prāṇa, kuṇḍalinī,* meditative states), and the tantric and yogic techniques, not given in the earlier upaniṣads, to attain them. Therefore, they are regarded as a significant integration of Vedanta and Tantra, which were previously considered incompatible. They are classified as 'minor' only because they postdate Ādi Śaṅkara.

Although their teachings actually predate Patañjali, the Yoga Upaniṣads were codified after the *Yoga Sūtras of Patañjali,* and form an important part of the classical yoga literature. However, they contain no references to Patañjali or his *Yoga Sūtras*. So, although the compilation of the Yoga Upaniṣads is post-Patañjali, the *vidyās*, or meditative disciplines, contained within them are pre-Patañjali. The Yoga Upaniṣads emerged at a time when the vedic and tantric cultures were coming together to share their knowledge. The wise thinkers from each culture sat down together and discussed how their insights and teachings could be combined in order to benefit humanity. Thus these upanisads combine the teachings of both tantra and yoga. It is evident in them that yoga leads to vedānta, and vedānta leads to yoga. However, they were written down by vedantic scholars and practitioners in order to show that these *vidyās* and related practices were not borrowed from Patañjali, but were known and practised from the ancient period.

Within the twenty-one Yoga Upaniṣads are six sub-groups which have their own main focus. The *Bindu Upaniṣads*, which include the *Amṛta-Bindu* (also known as the *Brahma-Bindu-Upaniṣad*), *Amṛta-Nada-Bindu*, *Nada-Bindu*, *Dhyāna-Bindu* and *Tejo-Bindu-Upaniṣads*, all concentrate on the bindu, the source or origin of all sound, and hence of creation. Bindu represents the transcendental sound manifested in the mantra *Aum*. The *Hamsa-Mantra*, *Soham*, is the main practice of the *Hamsa*, *Brahma-Vidya*, *Mahavakya* and *Paśupata-Brahma-Upaniṣads*. Concentration on *prāṇa*, the life force related to the process of inhalation and exhalation, brings the yogin to the knowledge of the transcendental self. The light of pure consciousness, which the enlightened irradiate is the theme of the *Advaya-Taraka* and *Maṅḍala-Brahmana-Upaniṣads*. The *Kṣurika-Upaniṣad* (*kṣurika* meaning 'dagger') emphasises non-attachment as a means to liberation. The sixth group, comprised of eight late Yoga Upaniṣads from 1200 to 1300 A.D., covers teachings related to hatha and kundalini yogas. They are the *Yoga-Kuṅḍalī, Yoga-Tattwa, Yoga-Śikhā, Varāha, Śāndilya, Tri-Śikhi-Brahmana, Yoga-Darśana* and *Yoga-Cūdāmani Upaniṣads.*

**Yoga Kuṇḍali Upaniṣad**

The teachings provided in this text on *kuṇḍalinī yoga* are totally original and unique. They were given by an experienced master, whose name is never mentioned, and who lived in an earlier period when such knowledge of yoga prevailed. The text is arranged in three parts. Chapter one contains the yogic physiology of kuṇḍalinī and the requisite disciplines necessary to undertake her activation and awakening. It begins with a relevant discussion on the two main ways to bring about an awakening: *citta*, expansion of consciousness, or prāṇa, liberation of energy. Kuṇḍalinī yoga belongs to the latter, but also accomplishes the former, which also demonstrates its tantric influence.

The disciplines required for kuṇḍalinī yoga include *mitāhāra*, moderation in diet, and the practice of *āsana*, specifically *padmāsana* and *vajrāsana*. These are followed by a thorough section on *prāṇāyāma*, or *kumbhaka*, which details the four major techniques: *suryabheda, ujjāyī, śītalī* and *bhastrikā*. The practice of *śakticāla*, an important method of kuṇḍalinī yoga, is described here in detail. This is an original practice, which cannot be found elsewhere. There is also an in-depth discussion on the *kuṇḍalinī śakti* herself, and what she really is. These are followed by the practices of the three *bandhas*: *mūlabandha, uddhiyāna,* and *jālandhara*, and their role in redirecting the energy upward to the brain.

These practices are followed by a detailed explanation of the ten obstructions, which arise on the path of higher yoga, and prevent the practitioner from achieving his or her goal. Then the process of kuṇḍalinī awakening is described and the practice is given, whereby it can be accomplished. The theory and rechannelling of *amṛta*, or immortal nectar, is further detailed to complete the process. The first chapter ends with the detailed practice of the *kuṇḍalinī śakti*, rising up the *suṣumnā*, piercing the three *granthis*, or psychic knots, and the six *cakras*, to unite with her Lord at *sahasrāra*, the crown centre.

Chapter two contains an exposition of *khecarī mudrā*, as it was known to and practised by the yogīs of old. Its importance as a practice leading to enlightenment, esoteric details and benefits are described here, along with the entire method, which is not found in modern books on yoga. The science of *khecarī* is followed by an explanation of *sūtra neti*. This is given as an adjunct to *khecarī mudrā*, in order to enhance the final awakening of *kuṇḍalinī* through the higher stages of *suṣumnā*.

Chapter three contains more specific instructions on how to maintain a higher *sādhana*. The auspicious days of practice are included, along with the necessity of renunciation. The two principles of creation, manas and *śakti*, are discussed, so that the *sādhaka* understands the basis of human bondage, which relates to identification with *śakti*, name and form. The practice of kuṇḍalinī yoga is further delineated in five precise steps. The *cakras* are described as the stairway to enlightenment and a major aspect of kuṇḍalinī yoga. The importance of yoga, guru and *sādhana* is explained. The chapter describes several important meditation practices: (i) on sound and *Soham*, (ii) on the *ātman*, (iii) spontaneous *jñāna yoga*, and (iv) merging with the *ātman*. Finally the master tells how to become a supreme yogī.

**References**

Saraswati, Swami Satyadharma. *Yoga Chudamani Upanishad* (Yoga Publications Trust, Munger, Bihar, India, 2003)

Aiyar, N.K. *Thirty Minor Upanishads* (Parimal Publications, Delhi, India 2009)

Feuerstein, Georg and Kak, Subhash and Frawley, David. *In Search of the Cradle of Civilization* (Quest Books, Illinois, USA 2001)

1. *ibidem* p.20

Feuerstein, Georg. *The Yoga Tradition* (Hohm Press, Prescott, Arizona USA 2001

Frawley, David. *Gods, Sages and Kings* (Passage Press, Salt Lake City, Utah USA 1991)

# योगकुण्डल्युपनिषत्
# Yogakuṇḍalyupaniṣat

## Invocation

योगकुण्डल्युपनिषद्योगसिद्धिहृदासनम् ।
निर्विशेषब्रह्मतत्त्वं स्वमात्रमिति चिन्तये ।
ॐ सह नाववत्विति शान्तिः ॥

*yogakuṇḍalyupaniṣadyogasiddhihṛdāsanam*
*nirviśeṣabrahmatattvam svamātramiti cintaye*
*Om saha nāvavatviti śāntiḥ*

**Anvay**
*iti*: thus; *cintaye*: I meditated on; *hṛd-āsanam*: seat of the heart; *yoga-siddhi*: power of yoga; *yoga-kuṇḍalī-upaniṣat*: upaniṣad of yoga kuṇḍalī; *svamātram*: being nothing but; *nirviśeṣa*: undiscriminating; *brahma-tattvam*: true knowledge of Brahma; *iti*: saying; *avavatu*: may [it] help; *nau*: both of us; *saha*: together; *śāntiḥ*: peace.

**Translation**
Thus I meditated on the seat of the heart, [which is] the power of yoga, on the upaniṣad of yoga kuṇḍalī, being nothing but the undiscriminating, true knowledge of Brahma. Saying: Om, may this teaching benefit both of us together. Peace.

**Invocation**
This invocation is chanted by the rishi or seer of the *Yoga Kuṇḍalī Upaniṣad,* to ensure that the teachings of this text may be revealed by the teacher to the student in a way most auspicious and beneficial to both. Before undertaking the

study of this text, the rishi says that he meditated on the seat of the heart, which is the centre of wisdom, where the soul resides. Being the seat of the soul, the heart is also the power of yoga. The purpose of yoga is ultimately to merge the individual soul with the cosmic soul, or consciousness, and this process of union begins at the heart. During his meditation, the rishi realised that the teaching given in this upaniṣad is nothing but the true knowledge of Brahma, the universal creative potential, which is one with all existence and beyond all qualification and discrimination.

# Chapter One

## प्रथमोऽध्यायः ।।

*prathamo 'dhyāyaḥ*

### Verse 1: Two causes of citta

हेतद्वयं हि चित्तस्य वासना च समीरणः ।
तयोर्विनष्ट एकस्मिंस्तद्द्वावपि विनश्यतः ।।१।।

*hetadvayaṃ hi cittasya vāsanā ca samīraṇaḥ*
*tayorvinaṣṭa ekasmiṃstaddvāvapi vinaśyataḥ* (1)

**Anvay**
*heta-dvayam*: two causes; *cittasya*: of individual consciousness; *vāsanā ca samīraṇaḥ*: mental disposition and vital energy; *ekasmin tayoḥ*: if one of these two; *vinaṣṭaḥ*: is destroyed; *api dvau*: then both; *vinaśyataḥ*: are destroyed.

**Translation**
The two causes of individual consciousness [are] the mental disposition and vital energy. If one of these two is destroyed, then both are destroyed.

**Commentary**
*Citta* is the individual consciousness. It is also referred to as the subconscious, individual mind, or mind-stuff, and the store-house of memory, or *saṃskāra*. Citta is one of the four parts of the *antaḥkaraṇa,* inner instrument of the consciousness. The four aspects of antaḥkaraṇa are: (i) *manas*, mind; (ii) *buddhi*, intellect; (iii) *citta*, subconscious; and *(iv) ahaṃkāra* or ego. Saṃskāras are the impressions of actions embedded in the subconscious mind. These stored impressions become our memories, and they condition the mind to think, feel and behave in particular patterns

throughout our lives.

*Vāsanās* are the deep rooted desires, which we carry with us over many lifetimes. These deep desires motivate our actions and ultimately create bondage, due to identification with and attachment to the desired object, person or place. We are born with certain fixed, deep rooted desires, which determine our character, qualities, habits, interests, opportunities and abilities. In a sense, it is the vāsanā that define our nature and destiny, and set out what we can and cannot, will and will not do or be, for the duration of our lives.

The mind draws on the saṃskāra, or memories, in order to better understand how to go about fulfilling the vāsanās in one's given situation in life. This requires the process of thinking or contemplation. Thinking is also an action, and it requires *prāṇa*, or life force, in order to carry out this process efficiently. Once the mind comes to a decision and formulates a plan, then *karma*, or action, will follow. Any action, whether the determination to act or the physical movement required to act, requires prāṇa. In the absence of prāṇa, there can be no life, no thought, no action.

Therefore, the two causes of citta are vāsanā and prāṇa. Both must work together in order to fulfil the purpose and destiny of each individual. It is an important tenet of yoga that, if one of these two can be eliminated, then the other will also be destroyed. Maybe this is the point where yoga first began. Because the yogis of old were not so interested in enhancing the body and mind, as we are today, but in transcending their conditioning and limitations. They had the supreme desire to merge the individual consciousness with the transcendental, and experience the totality of consciousness.

Here, in the first verse of this upaniṣad, we are given the two ways to achieve this: one by eliminating the deep-rooted desires, and the other by controlling the prāṇa.

## Verses 2 and 3a: Control of prāṇa

तयोरादौ समीरस्य जय कुर्यान्नरः सदा ।

मिताहारश्चासनं च शक्तिचालस्तृतीयकः ॥२॥

एतेषां लक्षनं वक्ष्ये शृणु गौतम सादरम् ।३।

*tayorādau samīrasya jaya kuryānnaraḥ sadā*
*mitāhāraścāsanaṃ ca śakticālastṛtīyakaḥ* (2)
*eteṣāṃ lakṣanaṃ vakṣye śṛṇu gautama sādaram* (3a)

**Anvay**
*tayoḥ*: of these two; *naraḥ*: man; *ādau*: at first; *sadā*: always; *kuryāt jaya*: should have control; *samīrasya*: of the *prāṇa; mitāhāraḥ*: sparing diet; *āsanam*: posture; *ca*: and; *tṛtīyakaḥ*: thirdly; *śakticālaḥ*: rotation and control of pranic force; *vakṣye*: I shall describe; *lakṣanam*: characteristics; *eteṣām*: of these; *śṛṇu*: listen; *sādaram*: attentively; *gautama*: Gautama.

**Translation**
Of these two, a man should always control the prāṇa first (by) moderation in diet, (second) posture and thirdly, rotation and control of the pranic force. I shall describe the characteristics of these. Listen attentively, Gautama.

**Commentary**
Here, we are given the easiest method to transcend the mind, which is control of the prāṇa. Rooting out the vāsanā is a very laborious job. The deep desires grow like weeds in a field, and the roots of each vāsanā are so deep that it is difficult to pull them out root and all. Some remnant of the root always remains, and then grows back again, when the time and situation are conducive for its expression. Furthermore, each vāsanā becomes the cause for new vasanas to grow and develop around it. So, the job goes on and on.

This is the difficulty of meditation, and all mind-orientated practices; whereas, control of the pranic force can be accomplished more easily. There are specific methods, which are given in yoga for this purpose. This verse enumerates three such methods: (i) *mitāhāra,* dietary control, (ii) *āsana*, control of posture, and (iii) *śakticāla*, control of the pranic force by rotation. These three are further described in the following verses.

## Verse 3b and 4a: Mitāhāra, moderation in diet

सुस्निग्धमधुराहारश्चतुर्थंशविवर्जितः ।।३।।

भुज्यते शिवसंप्रीत्यै मिताहारः स उच्यते ।४।

*susnigdhamadhurāhāraścaturthaṃśavivarjitaḥ* (3b)
*bhujyate śivasaṃprītyai mitāhāraḥ sa ucyate* (4a)

**Anvay**

*susnigdha*: soft; *madhura*: sweet; *āharaḥ*: offering; *bhujyate*: should be consumed; *vivarjitaḥ*: without filling; *caturthaṃśa*: one fourth; *śivas-aṃprītyai*: in order to please Śiva; *sa ucyate*: this is called; *mitāhāraḥ*: moderation in diet.

**Translation**

A soft, sweet offering should be consumed, without filling one fourth [of the stomach] in order to please Śiva. This is called moderation in diet.

**Commentary**

We can understand the importance of diet, when we observe our society today, There are so many different diets available, which people try to follow for their own purposes and needs. Yogic diet is another type of diet, where the emphasis is on *sattvic* food, for the purpose of maintaining a regular sādhana, or yogic practice. Yogic diet incorporates pure and balanced nutrition, which is neither too much nor too little, overcooked nor undercooked; which is fresh, and available locally and seasonally. The yogis of old generally consumed foods that were fresh, because there was no cold storage, fridges and freezers, as we have today. They also ate foods that were available locally and seasonally, because long distance transport, preservation and packaging were minimal.

Here, the verse recommends sweet and soft foods, meaning those items which are not bitter, salty, astringent or piquant, Yogic diet should be simple and consist of only one or two items per meal. It should be bland to the taste, so that it does not excite or upset the system or cause overeating. It should be soft, so that it does not require excess energy to break down and assimilate. A yogi considers the food that is consumed as an offering, which is made to the digestive fire and transmuted into energy for the life of the body and the evolution of consciousness.

Mitāhāra, moderation in diet, is also a measurement of discipline and self-control, whereby the yogi does not eat until the stomach is full. Rather, at the end of the meal, the stomach should always remain one fourth empty. When the stomach is filled to capacity, a state of *tamas*, or lethargy follows, which is not conducive to yogic practice. Therefore, the amount of food consumed is reduced, and this is done to please Śiva, the transcendental consciousness, which is the ultimate goal of yoga.

## Verses 4b to 6: Āsana, posture

आसनं द्‌विविधं प्रोक्तं पद्‌मं वज्रासनं तथा ।।४।।

ऊर्वोरुपरि चेद्‌धत्ते उभे पादतले यथा ।

पद्‌मासनं भवेदेतत्सर्वपापप्रणाशनम् ।।५।।

वामाङ्घ्रिमूलकन्दाधो ह्यन्यं तदुपरि क्षिपेत् ।

समग्रीवशिरः कायो वज्रासनमितीरितम् ।।६।।

*āsanaṃ dvividhaṃ proktaṃ padmaṃ vajrāsanaṃ tathā* (4b)
*ūrvorupari ceddhatte ubhe pādatale yathā*
*padmāsanaṃ bhavedetatsarvapāpapraṇāśanam* (5)
*vāmāṅghrimūlakandādho hyanyaṃ tadupari kṣipet*
*samagrīvaśiraḥ kāyo vajrāsanamitīritam* (6)

**Anvay**
*tathā*: then; *āsanam*: posture; *proktam*: is declared; *dvividham*: of two kinds; *bhavet*: it is; *padmāsanam*: lotus posture; *cet*: if; *ubhe pādatale*: both soles of the feet; *dhatte*: are placed; *upari*: on top of; *ūrvoḥ*: thighs; *etat*: this; *praṇāśanam*: destroys; *sarva-pāpa*: all sins; *iti īritam*: it is said; *vajrāsanam*: thunderbolt posture; *kṣipet*: one places; *vāma-anghri*: opposite foot; *mūlakanda-adhaḥ*: below the *mūlakanda*; *anyam*: other; *tat-upari*: above it; *grīva*: neck; *śiraḥ*: head; *kāyaḥ*: body; *sama*: upright.

**Translation**
Then posture is declared [to be] of two kinds: *padma* [and] *vajra*. It is *padmāsana* if both soles of the feet are placed on top of the thighs; this destroys all sins. It is said [to be] *vajrāsana* [when] one places the opposite foot below the *mūlakanda*, the other above it, the neck, head [and] body upright.

**Commentary**
In order to control the prāṇa, three methods were given above. The first being mitāhāra, or moderation in diet, and now the second, āsana or posture. The early yogis did not consider

āsana to be an end in itself, and they did not have a variety of āsana to choose from, as we know today, such as dynamic, static, forward bending, backward bending, inverted, balancing, and so on. Ordinarily, the body requires frequent movement, so we go on changing our position, or we reach for something or get up and walk somewhere. Āsana were regarded as postures in which the body could remain still, without the slightest movement, for long periods of time. For this purpose, two kinds of āsana are recommended in this teaching: *padma* and *vajra*.

### *Padmāsana*

Padmāsana is the 'lotus posture'. The lotus flower is regarded as a symbol of purity because, although it blooms on top of the water, its petals always remain dry. In the same way, the yogi is one who lives in the world, but remains untouched by it. Padmāsana is described here as sitting with both feet placed on top of the thighs. This posture can only be performed by practitioners with very flexible knees and ankles. The method is as follows:

Sit with both legs stretched forward in front of the body. Bend the right knee and place the right foot on top of the left thigh, so that the sole is turned upward and the heel is close to the pubic bone. In the same way, bend the left knee and place the left foot on top of the right thigh.

In the final position both knees should touch the ground. The spine, neck and head should be upright and straight. Relax the arms, and make sure that the shoulders are not hunched forward or raised. Close the eyes and observe the balance and alignment of the whole body.

Padmāsana is the most balanced posture, when it is performed correctly. Perfect alignment indicates that the posture is correct. Padmāsana is also a locked posture, which can hold the body steady and still for long durations of time.

While the body remains still, the mind becomes still. When the body and mind remain still, *suṣumnā,* the spiritual channel located at the center of the spinal column, opens. Padmāsana then directs the flow of prāṇa from the lower *cakras*, or psychic centers, upward through the suṣumnā pathway, to *sahasrāra* cakra, at the crown of the head. In this way, higher meditative states can be achieved spontaneously, by sitting in this posture alone.

### *Vajrāsana or siddhāsana*

Vajrāsana is the 'thunderbolt posture'. *Vajra* is also a major *nāḍī,* or energy channel, connected with the uro-genital system, which regulates the sexual energy. Today, we have several variations of this posture, such as sitting with both knees bent, so that the lower legs are beneath the upper legs and the buttocks sits in-between the feet. In early times, however, vajrāsana was also known as *guptāsana*, the 'secret pose'. In modern times, guptāsana is better known as *siddhāsana*, the 'perfect pose'. In the *Haṭha Yoga Pradīpika,* a classical text on yoga, (chapter 1, verse 37) it says that "Siddhāsana is also known as vajrāsana; some call it muktāsana and lastly it is called guptāsana." Therefore, we are describing the method here for siddhāsana, which is as follows:

Sit with both legs extended in front of the body. Bend the right knee and place the right sole against the left inner thigh. Bring the right heel underneath the body, so that it presses the perineum, midway between the genitals and the anus. Bend the left knee, and push the toes into the area between the right calf and thigh. Place the left ankle directly over the right ankle, so that the left heel is above the right heel. The left heel should also press the pubic bone, so that the genitals are in-between the two heels. Finally, grasp the right toes, and pull them up between the left calf and thigh.

In the final posture, the body weight rests on the right heel.

Make sure that the pressure of the right heel is firmly applied. The legs are both in a locked position, with the knees touching the ground. The spine, neck and head should remain upright and straight.

This posture also directs the sexual energy upward from the lower psychic centers. The position of the right foot at the perineum activates *mūlādhāra* cakra, while the left foot at the pubis activates *swādhiṣṭhāna*. The energy from these centers is then redirected up the suṣumnā for the purpose of higher meditation.

## Verses 7 to 10a: Śakticāla, raising the kuṇḍalinī

कुण्डल्येव भवेच्छक्तिस्तां तु संचालयेद्बुध ।
स्वस्थानाभा भ्रुवोर्मध्यं शक्तिचालनमुच्यते ॥७॥
तत्साधने द्वयं मुख्यं सरस्वत्सास्तु चालनम् ।
प्राणरोधमथाभ्यासादृज्वी कुण्डलिनी भवेत् ॥८॥
तयोरादौ सरस्वत्याश्चालनं कथयामि ते ।
अरुन्धत्येव कथिता पुराविद्भिः सरस्वती ॥९॥
यस्याः संचालनेनैव स्वयं चलति कुण्डली ।१०।

*kuṇḍalyeva bhavecchaktistāṃ tu saṃcālayedbudha*
*svasthānābhā bhruvormadhyaṃ śakticālanamucyate* (7)
*tatsādhane dvayaṃ mukhyaṃ sarasvatsāstu cālanam*
*prāṇarodhamathābhyāsādṛjvī kuṇḍalinī bhavet* (8)
*tayorādau sarasvatyāścālanaṃ kathayāmi te*
*arundhatyeva kathitā purāvidbhiḥ sarasvatī* (9)
*yasyāḥ saṃcālanenaiva svayaṃ calati kuṇḍalī* (10a)

**Anvay**

*śaktiḥ*: śakti; *bhavet*: is; *eva*: really; *kuṇḍalī*: kuṇḍalinī; *budhaḥ*: wise person; *tām saṃcālayet*: should move it up to; *svasthā-nābhā*: location [at] the navel; *bhruvormadhyam*: eyebrow centre; *ucyate*: is called; *śakticālanam*: raising the śakti; *tat sādhane*: to achieve this; *dvayam*: two; *mukhyam*: essential; *sarasvat-cālanam*: *sarasvaticāla*; *prāṇa-rodham*: control of prāṇa; *atha*: then; *ābhyāsāt*: through practice; *kuṇḍalinī bhavet*: kuṇḍalinī becomes; *ṛjvī* : straight; *tayoḥ*: of these two; *kathayāmi*: I shall describe; *te*: to you; *ādau*: first; *sarasvatyāścālanam*: sarasvatīcāla; *kathitā*: it is told; *purāvidbhiḥ*: by those who know the past; *sarasvatī*: Sarasvatī; *eva*: really; *arundhatī*: Arundhatī; *eva*: only; *saṃcālanena yasyāḥ*: by arousing her; *calati kuṇḍalī*: will kuṇḍalī arise; *svayam*: spontaneously.

**Translation**

Śakti is really kuṇḍalinī. A wise person should move it up [from] its location [to] the navel [and] to the eyebrow centre. [This] is called *śakticāla*. To achieve this, two [things] are essential: *sarasvatīcāla* [and] control of prāṇa. Then, through practice, the kuṇḍalinī becomes straight. Of these two, I shall describe to you first sarasvatīcāla. It is told by those who know the past [that] Sarasvatī [is] really Arundhatī. Only by arousing her will kuṇḍalinī arise spontaneously.

**Commentary**

According to yoga and tantra, *Śakti* is the universal energy that is inherent in consciousness and that brings about all of creation. The above verse states that śakti is really *kuṇḍalinī*. In this sense, kuṇḍalinī is the evolutionary energy, the creative potential of śakti in all beings, whether sentient or insentient. The word kuṇḍalinī comes from the root *kuṇḍa*, meaning a 'pit', such as a *havan* kuṇḍa, or a 'deeper place' such as a pond or lake. In human beings the kuṇḍalinī brings about individual creation by depositing the *cakra*, or psychic energy centers, and then descending downward through them, from the cosmic level at *sahasrāra*, the crown center, to *mūlādhāra*, the earthly or mundane level, at the perineum.

While the kuṇḍalinī descends through the cakra in order to create our manifest being, she is the evolutionary potential, transforming her cosmic potential into earthly existence. At every level, or cakra, the kuṇḍalinī deposits part of herself. These parts then combine to become the elements of our existence, starting with individual consciousness (*ajña cakra* at the mid-brain), and then space (*viśuddhi cakra* behind the throat), air (*anāhata cakra* behind the heart), fire (*maṇipura cakra* behind the navel), water (*swādhiṣṭhāna cakra*, behind the pubis) and finally earth (*mūlādhāra cakra* at the perineum). Each of these elements is stored in the relevant cakra, as a part of our core energy, for the duration of our life.

Having completed her descent from the unmanifest into the manifest dimension of existence, the kuṇḍalinī rests for a while in a dormant state at the mūlādhāra cakra, the root center, which equates to a deeper place. While resting, her cosmic, kinetic force becomes contracted and coiled, like a serpent, which sleeps inside the earth. During this dormant phase of creation, the kuṇḍalinī dreams our life on Earth, and we experience this earthly existence as if it were very real, very permanent, very important. Upon completion of this dormant phase, however, the kuṇḍalinī begins to awaken, to rise up, in order to return back to the source of her existence.

At this point in our evolution, the spiritual phase begins. The kuṇḍalinī slowly unwinds her coils, and stretches herself back up through the cakra, on her return journey to the cosmic dimension of consciousness. As she moves upward, from cakra to cakra, she raises the consciousness that had descended into the earthly existence along with her, and dissolves all the identifications and illusions of material life. In this way, she ultimately becomes our spiritual path and guides our consciousness back through higher and subtler states. Hence, the significance of kuṇḍalinī is actually three-fold. She is the creator, the sustainer, and also the dissolver of our individual being or nature. Like a mother, she brings us into this world, then patiently allows us to experience it fully, and finally returns us back to our spirit nature.

Hence, the teaching continues, that a wise person should move the kuṇḍalinī upward, from its location at the mūlādhāra cakra, the base, to maṇipura cakra, behind the navel, and then to ajña cakra behind the eyebrow center. This upward movement of the kuṇḍalinī energy is called *śakticāla.* In order to achieve this, there are two essential practices: *sarasvatīcāla* and control of prāṇa. Saraswatī is another name for *suṣumnā*, the subtle spiritual channel at the center of the spinal column. Sarasvatīcāla refers to the awakening of suṣumnā, and śakticāla to raising the kuṇḍalinī energy up the suṣumnā.

In most people, the suṣumnā channel remains closed and dormant. Only by awakening suṣumnā can the kuṇḍalinī arise spontaneously. Suṣumnā can be opened by controlling and equalising the prāṇa in *iḍā* and *piṅgalā nāḍīs*, the two major energy channels, which carry the mental and vital energies respectively. This is achieved by moderation of diet, yogic postures, and rotation of the prāṇa and the breath. Then, by regular practice, the kuṇḍalinī force begins to awaken and uncoil itself. In order for this cosmic potential to stretch out and straighten herself, she must first enter the mouth of suṣumnā, situated just above the mūlādhāra cakra, and rise up to maṇipura cakra and then ajña cakra. From ajña cakra the final upward movement of kuṇḍalinī to sahasrāra cakra takes place effortlessly.

The teacher further adds that those persons, who know the history of the past, also consider saraswati to be the same as Arundhatī, the esteemed and spiritually awakened wife of Rishi Vaśiṣṭha, who was one of the *sapta rishis*, the seven most venerated seers of ancient India. Arundhatī is respected, even today, for her chastity as well as learning. Her qualities are also seen to be those of saraswatī, or suṣumnā, nāḍī. Being the spiritual channel in the human body, suṣumnā holds all knowledge, and is beyond worldly desire. Arundhatī was said to be fully awakened, and her name comes from the root *arundhi*, meaning 'to arise', 'to ascend'. When the kuṇḍalinī rises to the crown centre, one is said to be fully awakened.

**Verses 10b to 18: Method of śakticāla**

यस्याः संचालनेनैव स्वयं चलति कुण्डली ।
इडायां वहति प्राणे बद्ध्वा पद्मासनं दृढम् ।।१०।।
द्वादशाङ्गुलदैर्घ्यं च अम्बरं चतुरङ्गुलम् ।
विस्तीर्य तेन तनानाडीं वेष्टयित्वा ततः सुधीः ।।११।।
अङ्गुष्ठतर्जनीभ्यां तु हस्ताभ्यां धारयेद्द्वढम् ।
स्वशक्त्या चालयेद्वामे दक्षिणेन पुनःपुनः ।।१२।।
मुहूर्तद्वयपर्यन्तं निर्भयाच्चालयेत्सुधीः ।
ऊर्ध्वमाकर्षयेत्किंचित्सुषुम्नां कुण्डलीगताम् ।।१३।।
तेन कुण्डलिनी तस्याः सुषुम्नाया मुखं व्रजेत् ।
जहाति तस्मात्प्राणोऽयं सुषुम्नां व्रजति स्वतः ।।१४।।
तुन्दे तु तानं कुर्याच्च कण्ठसंकोचने कृते ।
सरस्वत्यां चालनेन वक्षसश्चोर्ध्वगो मरुत् ।।१५।।
सूर्येण रेचयेद्वायुं सरस्वत्यास्तु चालने ।
कण्ठसंकोचनं कृत्वा वक्षसश्चोर्ध्वगो मरुत् ।।१६।।
तस्मात्संचालयेन्नित्यं शब्दगर्भा सरस्वतीम् ।
यस्याः संचालनेनैव योगी रोगैः प्रमुच्यते ।।१७।।
गुल्मं जलोदरः प्लीहा ये चान्ये तुन्दमध्यगाः ।
सर्वे ते शक्तिचालेन रोगा नायन्ति निश्चयम् ।।१८।।

*iḍāyāṃ vahati prāṇe baddhvā padmāsanaṃ dṛḍham* (10b)
*dvādaśāṅguladairghyaṃ ca ambaraṃ caturaṅgulam*
*vistīrya tena tanānāḍīṃ veṣṭayitvā tataḥ sudhīḥ* (11)
*aṅguṣṭhatarjanībhyāṃ tu hastābhyāṃ dhārayeddvaḍham*
*svaśaktyā cālayedvāme dakshiṇena punaḥpunaḥ* (12)
*muhūrtadvayaparyantaṃ nirbhayāccālayetsudhīḥ*
*ūrdhvamākarṣayetkiṃcitsuṣumnāṃ kuṇḍalīgatām* (13)
*tena kuṇḍalinī tasyāḥ suṣumnāyā mukhaṃ vrajet*

*jahāti tasmātprāṇo 'yam suṣumnāṃ vrajati svataḥ* (14)
*tunde tu tānaṃ kuryācca kaṇṭhasaṃkocane kṛte*
*sarasvatyāṃ cālanena vakṣasaścordhvago marut* (15)
*sūryeṇa recayedvāyuṃ sarasvatyāstu cālane*
*kaṇṭhasaṃkocanaṃ kṛtvā vakṣasaścordhvago marut* (16)
*tasmātsaṃcālayennityaṃ śabdagarbhā sarasvatīm*
*yasyāḥ saṃcālanenaiva yogī rogaiḥ pramucyate* (17)
*gulmaṃ jalodaraḥ plīhā ye cānye tundamadhyagāḥ*
*sarve te śakticālena rogā nāyanti niścayam* (18)

**Anvay**

*prāṇe*: when the prāṇa; *vahati*: passes; *iḍāyāṃ*: through ida; *sudhīḥ*: wise man; *dṛḍham*: firmly; *baddhvā*: bound; *padmāsanam*: padmāsana; *vistīrya*: having expanded; *nāḍīm*: nāḍī; *dairghyam*: length; *dvādaśa-aṅgula*: twelve fingers; *ca*: and; *ambaram*: circumference; *catuḥ-aṅgulam*: four fingers; *dhārayet*: he should hold; *tanā*: continually; *veṣṭayitvā*: enclosing; *aṅguṣṭha-tarjanībhyām*: with the thumb [and] forefingers; *dvadham hastābhyām*: of both hands; *punaḥpunaḥ*: repeatedly; *cālayet*: stir up; *svaśaktyā*: śakti; *dakshiṇena vāme*: from right to left; *sudhīḥ*: wise man; *cālayet*: stir up; *nirbhayāt*: fearlessly; *paryantam*: for the duration; *muhūrta-dvaya*: two muhūrtas (48 minutes); *ākarṣayet*: he should draw; *ūrdhvam*: upwards; *kiṃcit*: a little; *kuṇḍalī*: kuṇḍalinī; *gatām*: goes into; *suṣumnām*: *suṣumnā*, central nāḍī; *tena*: thus; *kuṇḍalinī*: kuṇḍalinī; *vrajet*: enters; *mukham*: mouth; *tasyāḥ suṣumnāyāḥ*: of the suṣumnā; *ayam prāṇaḥ*: the prāṇa; *jahāti*: departs; *tasmāt*: from there; *vrajati*: enters; *suṣumnām*: suṣumnā; *svataḥ*: of its own accord; *kuryāt tānam*: he should expand; *tunde*: abdomen; *saṃkocane kṛte*: by contracting; *kaṇṭha*: throat; *cālanena sarasvatyām*: by agitating in *sarasvatī*; *marut*: prāṇa; *ūrdhvagaḥ*: going upwards; *vakṣasaḥ*: chest; *vāyuṃ recayet*: he should exhale; *sūryeṇa*: through the right nostril; *āstu cālane sarasvatī*: continuing to agitate *sarasvatī*; *saṃkocanaṃ kṛtvā* : by contracting; *kaṇṭha*: throat; *marut*:

prāṇa; *ūrdhvagaḥ*: going upwards; *vakṣasaḥ*: chest; *tasmāt*: therefore; *nityam saṃcālayet sarasvatīm*: he should continually stir up sarasvatī; *garbhā*: womb; *śabda*: sound; *eva*: simply; *saṃcālanena yasyāḥ*: by arousing her; *yogī pramucyate*: yogin is freed; *rogaiḥ*: from disease; *gulmam*: *gulma*, disease of the spleen; *jalodaraḥ*: *jalodara*, dropsy; *plīhāḥ*: *plīha*, disease of the spleen; *ca*: and; *sarve anye rogāḥ*: all other diseases; *tunda-madhya-gāḥ*: arising within the abdomen; *niścayam*: certainly; *nāyanti*: are prevented; *śakticālena*: by *śakticāla.*

**Translation**

When the prāṇa passes through *iḍā*, [then] the wise man, firmly bound [in] padmāsana, having expanded the nāḍī the length [of] twelve fingers and circumference [of] four fingers, should hold [the lower ribs] continually enclosing [them] with the thumb [and] forefingers of both hands, [and] repeatedly stir up the śakti from right to left. The wise man should stir [it] up fearlessly for the duration [of] two muhūrtas. He should draw [it] upwards a little [so that] the kuṇḍalinī goes into *suṣumnā.*

Thus kuṇḍalinī enters the mouth of the suṣumnā. The prāṇa departs from there [and] enters suṣumnā of its own accord. He should expand the abdomen by contracting the throat. By agitating in *sarasvatī*, the prāṇa, going upwards, [reaches] the chest. He should exhale through the right nostril, [while] continuing to agitate *sarasvatī* [and] contracting the throat, the prāṇa goes upwards [from] the chest. Therefore he should continually stir up sarasvatī [whose] womb [is of] sound. Simply by arousing her, the yogin is freed from disease. Diseases of the spleen, dropsy, and all other diseases arising within the abdomen are certainly prevented by *śakticāla.*

***Technique: Arousing Śakti***

Sit in padmāsana, if it is comfortable for you, or in another locked meditative pose of your choice. Allow the body to become calm and still. Become aware of the natural breath. Breathe slowly and rhythmically without any effort or strain.

Become aware of suṣumnā nāḍī, the spiritual channel through which kuṇḍalinī arises. See it arising from a point below the coccyx and just above mūlādhāra cakra, and flowing upward through the center of the spinal column to the crown of the head. See the major cakras attached to suṣumnā, each in their proper place: mūlādhāra at the perineum, swādhiṣṭhāna at the coccyx, maṇipura behind the navel, anāhata behind the heart, viśuddhi behind the throat pit, and ajña at the mid-brain.
Next, begin to sense or to imagine the iḍā (mental) and piṅgalā (vital) energy channels, which arise from mūlādhāra cakra. See iḍā arising from the left of mūlādhāra, and piṅgalā from the right. These two energy channels spiral upward, merging with suṣumnā, and then crossing over at each cakra junction.

Focus on the pathway of iḍā, curving to the left from mūlādhāra and crossing swādhiṣṭhāna. From swādhiṣṭhāna, iḍā curves to the right and crosses maṇipura. From maṇipura, iḍā curves to the left and crosses anāhata. From anāhata, iḍā curves to the right and crosses viśuddhi. From viśuddhi, iḍā curves to the left and terminates at ajña.

Now imagine or feel a stream of prāṇaśakti, in the form of white light, passing through the iḍā pathway. See or feel the white light, expanding upward through iḍā for about twelve fingers, or nine inches, to the level of the maṇipura cakra. The width of the channel also expands with light to about four fingers, or three inches.

At this point, place both hands on the lower part of the ribcage, continually enclosing it, with the thumbs behind and the four fingers in front. Repeatedly stir up the prāṇaśakti fearlessly from left to right and right to left for as long as youfeel comfortable to do so. The duration can be gradually increased to a period of two hours. Draw the prāṇaśakti upward little by little, so that the kuṇḍalinī enters the suṣumnā channel at maṇipura cakra, behind the navel.

***Raising Śakti up suṣumnā***

When the kuṇḍalinī enters suṣumnā, the prāṇaśakti departs from ida nāḍī and enters suṣumnā of its own accord. Perform *jālandhara bandha*, the throat lock, by bending the head forward and contracting the throat. Simultaneously, expand and contract the abdomen, agitating the kuṇḍalinī in suṣumnā, so that it flows upward and reaches the anāhata cakra in chest region.

Become aware of the breath, flowing through the nostrils. Imagine or feel the breath flowing in through the left nostril and out through the right. Continue to perform jālandhara bandha, contraction of the throat, and agitate the kuṇḍalinī in suṣumnā, so that the kuṇḍalinī flows upward from anāhata cakra in the chest region to viśuddhi cakra behind the throat, and then to ajña cakra, at the mid-brain.

In this way, the yogi should continually stir up the kuṇḍalinī in suṣumnā, which is the womb of sound. Different subtle *nāda*, or psychic sounds, emanate from suṣumnā, such as bells, flute, conch, vina and so on. As the kuṇḍalinī ascends, these sounds can be heard from within the consciousness itself. By following these subtle sound vibrations, the kuṇḍalinī ascends through the cakra, and reaches bindu, at the top back of the head, and ultimately sahasrāra, at the crown.

Therefore, the yogi should continually stir up the kuṇḍalinī in suṣumnā. One is freed from disease simply by arousing the kuṇḍalinī and raising her through suṣumnā. Diseases of the spleen, the abdomen, dropsy and all other diseases are averted by the practice of śakticāla.

### Verses 19 to 21: Kumbhaka, retention of the breath

प्राणरोधमथेदानीं प्रवक्ष्यामि समासतः ।
प्राणश्च देहयो वायुरायामः कुम्भकः स्मृतिः ।।१९।।
स एव द्विविधः प्रोक्तः सहितः केवलस्तथा ।
यावत्केवलसिद्धिः स्यात्तावत्सहितमभ्यसेत् ।।२०।।
सूर्योज्जायी शीतली च भस्त्री चैव चतुर्थिका ।
भेदैरेव समं कुम्भो यः स्यात्सहितकुम्भकः ।।२१।।

*prāṇarodhamathedānīṃ pravakṣyāmi samāsataḥ*
*prāṇaśca dehayo vāyurāyāmaḥ kumbhakaḥ smṛtiḥ* (19)
*sa eva dvividhaḥ proktaḥ sahitaḥ kevalastathā*
*yāvatkevalasiddhiḥ syāttāvatsahitamabhyaset* (20)
*sūryojjāyī śītalī ca bhastrī caiva caturthikā*
*bhedaireva samaṃ kumbho yaḥ syātsahitakumbhakaḥ* (21)

**Anvay**

*atha idānīm*: so now; *pravakṣyāmi*: I shall explain; *samāsataḥ*: succinctly; *prāṇa-rodham*: suppression of prāṇa; *āyāmaḥ*: movement; *vāyuḥ*: air; *dehayaḥ*: in the body; *ca*: and; *smṛtiḥ*: is called; *kumbhakaḥ*: breath retention; *sa proktaḥ*: it is said; *eva*: just; *dvividhaḥ*: of two kinds; *sahitaḥ*: by practice; *kevalaḥ*: spontaneous, absolute; *yāvat . . . tāvat*: as long as; *abhyaset*: one practises; *sahitam*: by practice; *syāt*: one will have; *kevala-siddhiḥ*: power of absolute; *kumbhaḥ*: closing of the nostrils and mouth; *samam*: same; *caturthikā bhedaiḥ*: in the four parts; *eva*: namely; *sūrya ujjāyī śītalī ca bhastrī*: *sūrya, ujjāyī, śītalī* and *bhastrī*; *yaḥ syāt*: this is; *sahitakumbhakaḥ*: *sahita kumbhaka.*

**Translation**

So now, I shall explain succinctly the suppression of prāṇa. Prāṇa is the movement [of] vital air in the body and [its retention] is called *kumbhaka.* It is said [to be] just of two kinds, *sahita* and *kevala.* As long as he practises *sahita*, he will have the power of *kevala*. The closing of the nostrils and the mouth [is] the same in the four parts, namely *sūrya, ujjāyī, śītalī* and *bhastrī.* This is *sahita kumbhaka*.

**Commentary**

*Kumbhaka*, the retention of breath or prāṇa, is the basis of prāṇāyāma. Prāṇa is the vital energy or life force, constantly moving in all beings, and which also moves in and out with the breath. Ordinarily, the prāṇa of an individual moves throughout the body, and also flows outside, whenever the senses connect with people, places and things. Every interaction is an exchange of prāṇa. The practice of kumbhaka developed, because the yogis of old wished to conserve their prāṇa in order to awaken the consciousness.

The word kumbhaka comes from the root *kumbha*, meaning a 'vessel' or 'pot'. In order to retain the breath inside, the diaphragm expands, so that the belly forms a pot, where the air is stored for a duration of time. There are two types of kumbhaka: *sahita*, retention practised by intentionally holding the breath, and *kevala*, spontaneous breath retention. Sahita or intentional retention is also of two types: *antar kumbhaka*, where the breath is held inside, following inhalation, and *bahir kumbhaka*, where the breath is held outside, following exhalation.

The practice of sahita kumbhaka leads to kevala kumbhaka, where breath suspension takes place by itself, during deep meditation, as an alternate state of consciousness arises. During this state the pressure in the lungs becomes the same as the atmospheric pressure, allowing the respiratory process to cease and the lungs to stop their activity. When the breath ceases, the mind becomes totally still, and the veil that separates the mind from the higher consciousness is raised. Therefore, the most important aspect of prāṇāyāma is kumbhaka, and in the ancient texts prāṇāyāma is also known as kumbhaka.

In order to master kumbhaka, the yogi must gradually gain control over the breathing process. For this reason great emphasis has been placed on the inhalation and exhalation during prāṇāyāma practice. Control of the breath leads to control of prāṇa, and control of prāṇa leads to control of the mind. By regulating the flow of breath, one can calm the mind in preparation for higher meditation. Hence, the above verse states that the yogi, who practises sahita prāṇāyāma, will have the power of kevala, the power to transcend the mind and experience the pure consciousness.

Sahita kumbhaka involves the breathing process and extension of the breath, because it is practised; whereas, kevala kumbhaka, which arises spontaneously, does not. A number of prāṇāyāma practices are therefore included in the sahita category. The above verse mentions four methods: (i) *sūrya*, (ii) *ujjāyī*, (iii) *śītalī*, and (iv) *bhastrika*. Each of these practices involves a particular type of inhalation and exhalation, for the regulation of the prāṇas and the mind. However, all four utilise the same method of retention, so these comprise sahita kumbhaka.

## Verses 22 to 23: Preparation for kumbhaka

पवित्रे निर्जने देशे शर्करादिविवर्जिते ।

धनुःप्रमाणपर्यन्ते शीताग्निजलवर्जिते ।।२२।।

पवित्रे नात्युच्चनीचे ह्यासने सुखदे सखे ।

बद्धपद्मासनं कृत्वा सरस्वत्यास्तु चालनम् ।।२३।।

*pavitre nirjane deśe śarkarādivivarjite*
*dhanuḥpramāṇaparyante śītāgnijalavarjite* (22)
*pavitre nātyuccanīce hyāsana sukhade sakhe*
*baddhapadmāsanaṃ kṛtvā sarasvatyāstu cālanam* (23)

**Anvay**

*kṛtvā padmāsanam*: seated in *padmāsana*; *baddha*: firmly; *āsane*: on a seat; *sukhade*: pleasant; *sakhe*: favourable; *pavitre*: pure; *nāti*: not too; *uccanīce*: high or low; *deśe*: in a place; *pavitre*: sacred; *nirjane*: solitary; *vivarjite*: free from; *śarkara-ādi*: grit etc; *pramāṇa-paryante*: of the length; *dhanuḥ*: bow; *varjite*: without; *śīta*: cold; *agni*: fire; *jala*: water; *āstu*: one should remain; *cālanam sarasvatī*: stirring up sarasvatī.

**Translation**

Seated firmly in *padmāsana* on a pleasant [and] favourable seat [which is] pure [and] not too high or low, in a sacred [and] solitary place free from grit etc, of the length [of] a bow, without cold, fire [or] water, he should remain stirring up sarasvatī.

**Commentary**

In modern times prāṇāyāma is generally practised on a yoga mat or cushion, in a yoga room or studio. These verses describe how the yogis of old prepared for the practice. Being more flexible and used to sitting on the floor or the ground, they used the balanced and locked position of padmāsana, the lotus pose, which most yogis could maintain easily for long durations. They traditionally sat on a seat, which was not too high or too low. The seat should not be too high, so that if they entered a trance state during the practice, there was no chance of falling from the seat. The seat should not be too low, so that insects or rodents would not crawl on the body and disturb the practice.

The seat should also be favorable and pure, ie., sweet smelling, clean and comfortable to sit on. For this purpose they often placed a mound of special grasses, such as kusa grass, which was then covered by a deer skin and a soft clean cloth. The seat would be freshened each day with freshly cut grasses and a clean cloth, to maintain its purity. The seat measured about one metre, the length of a bow, and should be free from dirt or grit. A quiet and solitary place was chosen for the practice, generally in a forest under a spreading tree, on a river bank, in a secluded cave, or on the side of a hill. The most favorable and sacred place would be where another yogi had practised sādhana or tapasya and achieved higher states of meditation.

In such an auspicious setting, which is free from excessive cold or heat, fire or smoke, and which is dry and protected from the rain and sun, the yogi should remain seated, constantly stirring up the saraswatī, or raising the prāṇa up the suṣumnā nāḍī in preparation for the practice of prāṇāyāma.

## Verses 24 to 26a: Sūryabheda kumbhaka

दक्षनाड्या समाकृष्य बहिष्ठं पवनं शनैः ।

यथेष्टं पूरयेद्वायुं रेचयेदिडया ततः ।।२४।।

कपालशोधने वापि रेचयेत्पवनं शनैः ।

चतुष्कं वातदोषं तु कृमिदोषं निहन्ति च ।।२५।।

पुनः पुनरिदं कार्यं सूर्यभेदमुदाहृतम् ।२६।

*dakṣanāḍyā samākṛṣya bahiṣṭhaṃ pavanaṃ śanaiḥ*
*yatheṣṭaṃ pūrayedvāyuṃ recayediḍayā tataḥ* (24)
*kapālaśodhane vāpi recayetpavanaṃ śanaiḥ*
*catuṣkaṃ vātadoṣaṃ tu kṛmidoṣaṃ nihanti ca* (25)
*punaḥ punaridaṃ kāryaṃ sūryabhedadamudāhṛtam* (26a)

**Anvay**
*samākṛṣya*: having drawn in; *śanaiḥ*: slowly; *pavanam*: air; *bahiṣṭham*: from outside; *dakṣa-nāḍyā*: through the right nostril; *vāyuṃ pūrayet*: he should inhale; *yatheṣṭam*: for as long as he wants; *tataḥ*: then; *recayet*: exhale; *iḍayā*: through the left; *śodhane*: after purifying; *kapāla*: skull; *pavanam recayet*: he should exhale; *śanaiḥ*: slowly; *nihanti*: destroys; *catuṣkam*: four; *vāta-doṣam*: *vāta* diseases; *ca*: and; *kṛmi-doṣam*: disease of worms; *idam kāryam*: this should be done; *punaḥ punaḥ*: repeatedly; *tam udāhṛtam*: this is called; *sūryabheda*: *sūryabheda.*

**Translation**
Having slowly drawn in the air from outside through the right nostril, he should inhale for as long as he wants, [and] then exhale through the left [nostril]. After purifying the skull, he should exhale slowly. [This] destroys the four *vāta* diseases and the disease of worms. This should be done repeatedly. This is called *sūryabheda.*

**Commentary**
*Sūryabheda* is the first kumbhaka described here, although it

is not commonly taught nowadays. The word *sūrya* means 'sun', and in this context it refers to the vitalising power of the piṅgalā nāḍī. The word *bheda* means 'to pierce' or 'to pass through'. So, sūryabheda is a practice that activates the vital energy by piercing the piṅgalā nāḍī, which is associated with the flow of breath through the right nostril.

***Technique***
Sit in padmāsana or any comfortable meditation āsana. Allow the body to relax completely and the mind to become still. Become aware of the breath. Practice slow rhythmic breathing. While inhaling, raise the prāṇa with the breath up the suṣumnā pathway from mūlādhāra cakra (at the perineum) to maṇipura cakra (behind the navel). Hold the breath and the prāṇa at maṇipura for a few seconds. Exhale slowly and return the prāṇa from maṇipura to mūlādhāra through the suṣumnā. Go on activating the prāṇa in suṣumnā in this way until you feel the maṇipura cakra becoming vibrant and heated.

Raise the right hand in front of the face and close the left nostril with the ring finger. Inhale slowly through the right nostril, drawing the breath up the suṣumnā from manipura to ajña cakra at the mid-brain. Continue the inhalation for as long as comfortable. At the end of inhalation hold the breath at ajña, inside the cranium, for a few seconds and feel the energy purifying the cranium and skull.

Close the right nostril with the thumb and release the left nostril. Exhale slowly through the left nostril, descending back down the suṣumnā with the breath and energy from ajña to manipura chakra, behind the navel. This is one round. Continue the practice for ten to twenty rounds.

Sūryabheda kumbhaka activates the piṅgalā nāḍī by inhaling through the right nostril. However, this action is balanced by exhaling through the left nostril, which stimulates the iḍā nāḍī, associated with the mental or passive energy. By activating the vital and mental forces in this way, sūryabheda rebalances the three *doṣas*, or humours, in the body: *kapha* (mucus), *pitta* (acid or bile) and *vāta* (wind). Regular practice of this prāṇāyāma thereby removes the four vāta disorders: (i) gas and indigestion, (ii) constipation, (iii) nervousness and palsy, and (iv) anxiety and stress; along with the disease of worms.

## Verses 26b to 29: Ujjāyī kumbhaka

मुखं संयम्यं नाडिभ्यामाकृष्य पवनं शनैः ।।२६।।

यथा लगति कण्ठात्तु हृदयावधि सस्वनम् ।

पूर्ववत्कुम्भयेत्प्राणं रेचयेदिडया ततः ।।२७।।

शीर्षोदितानलहरं गलश्लेष्महरं परम् ।

सर्वरोगहरं पुण्यं देहानलविवर्धनम् ।।२८।।

नाडीजलोदरं धातुगतदोषविनाशनम् ।

गच्छतस्तिष्ठतः कार्यमुज्जायाख्यं तु कुम्भकम् ।।२९।।

*mukhaṃ samyamyaṃ nāḍibhyāmākṛṣya pavanaṃ śanaiḥ* (26b)
*yathā lagati kaṇṭhāttu hṛdayāvadhi sasvanam*
*pūrvavatkumbhayetprāṇaṃ recayediḍayā tataḥ* (27)
*śīrṣoditānalaharaṃ galaśleṣmaharaṃ param*
*sarvarogaharaṃ puṇyaṃ dehānalavivardhanam* (28)
*nāḍījalodaraṃ dhātugatadoṣavināśanam*
*gacchatastiṣṭhataḥ kāryamujjāyākhyaṃ tu kumbhakam* (29)

**Anvay**

*śanaiḥ*: slowly; *ākṛṣya*: drawing in; *pavanam*: breath; *nāḍibhyām*: through both nostrils; *mukham*: mouth; *samyamyam*: closed; *lagati*: he holds; *sasvanam*: its sound; *kaṇṭhāt*: from the throat; *hṛdaya-avadhi*: to the heart; *yathā*: as long as; *kumbhayet prāṇam*: he restrains the prāṇa; *pūrvavat*: as before; *tataḥ*: then; *recayet*: exhales; *iḍayā*: through the left; *haram*: destroys; *anala*: fire; *udita*: produced; *śīrṣa*: head; *śleṣma*: phlegm; *gala*: throat; *param*: afterwards; *sarva-roga*: all sicknesses; *vivardhanam*: increasing; *anala*: digestive power; *deha*: body; *puṇyam*: purifying; *vināśanam*: it removes; *doṣa*: diseases; *gata*: arising in; *nāḍī-jalodaram dhātu*: nāḍīs, *jalodara, dhātus*; *tu kumbhakam*: this kumbhaka; *ākhyam*: is called; *ujjāya*: ujjāyī; *kāryam*: is to be done; *gacchataḥ-tiṣṭhataḥ*: walking or standing.

**Translation**

Slowly drawing in the breath through both nostrils, mouth closed, he holds its sound from the throat to the heart as long as [he wishes]. He restrains the prāṇa as before, then exhales through the left [nostril]. [This] destroys the fire produced [in] the head, the phlegm [in] the throat [and] afterwards destroys all sicknesses, [thereby] increasing the digestive power [in] the body [and] purifying [it]. It removes diseases arising in the nāḍīs, *jalodara* [and] *dhātus.* This kumbhaka is called ujjāyī [and] is to be done walking or standing.

**Commentary**

*Ujjāyī* kumbhaka is a relaxing practice, also known as 'psychic breathing'. The word ujjāyī comes from the root *jaya,* meaning 'victorious'. This method can be done anywhere, even while standing or walking. However, it is useful to develop the practice while sitting, as it is very subtle and brings about a deep introverted state rapidly and effortlessly. Ujjāyī has been integrated into different meditation practices, such as japa and ajapa japa, because it takes place spontaneously, when the awareness enters deeper states of consciousness. It is an important adjunct to the practices of kriya yoga and prāṇa vidya, and may also be practised together with the techniques of haṭha yoga.

In ujjāyī, the upper region of the throat is contracted slightly, so that the breath produces a gentle snoring sound, like the breathing of a sleeping baby. This sound can be heard from within by the practitioner, but should not be forced or loud enough to be heard by others outside.

***Technique***

Sit in any comfortable meditation posture. Relax the entire body from head to toe. Feel the body becoming calm and still. Become aware of the natural breath. Begin to practise slow rhythmic breathing. Feel the smooth even flow of breath through both nostrils. Keep the mouth closed.

Slowly draw the breath in through both nostrils, while contracting the glottis slightly, so that a sonorous sound can be heard in the throat, Descend with the inhalation and the sound from the throat to the region of the heart. Retain the breath inside the chest for a comfortable duration.

Then, raising the right hand in front of the face, close the right nostril with the thumb. Exhale slowly through the left nostril, contracting the glottis. Ascend from the heart region to the throat with the ujjāyī exhalation and the sonorous sound. Practice ten to twenty rounds, or continue the practice for five to ten minutes.

The practice of ujjāyī calms the mind and alleviates anger, fear, stress and anxiety. It effectively removes phlegm from the throat and manages mucus-related disorders. It increases the digestive power and purifies the digestive tract, which helps to destroy all disease. It rebalances the nāḍīs, and removes disorders related with the energy flows. It manages conditions of water retention, such as dropsy and edema, and restores the body tissues and vital force.

## Verses 30 and 31: Śītalī kumbhaka

जिह्वया वायुमाकृष्य पूर्ववत्कुम्भकादनु ।
शनैस्तु घ्राणरन्ध्राभ्यां रेचयेदनिलं सुधीः ॥३०॥
गुल्मप्लीहादिकान्दोषान्क्षयं पित्तं ज्वरं तृषाम् ।
विषाणि शीतली नाम कुम्भकोऽयं निहन्ति च ॥३१॥

*jihvayā vāyumākṛṣya pūrvavatkumbhakādanu*
*śanaistu ghrāṇarandhrābhyāṃ recayedanilaṃ sudhīḥ* (30)
*gulmaplīhādikāndoṣānkṣayaṃ pittaṃ jvaraṃ tṛṣām*
*viṣāṇi śītalī nāma kumbhako 'yaṃ nihanti ca* (31)

**Anvay**
*ākṛṣya*: after drawing in; *vāyum*: breath; *jihvayā*: through the tongue; *anu*: then; *kumbhakāt*: retaining; *pūrvavat*: as before; *sudhīḥ*: wise man; *śanaiḥ*: slowly; *anilam recayet*: should exhale; *ghrāṇarandhrābhyām*: through both nostrils; *ayam kumbhakaḥ*: this breath retention; *nāma śītalī*: called *śītalī*; *nihanti kṣayam*: causes the removal; *doṣān*: diseases; *ādikān*: such as; *gulma plīha*: diseases of the spleen; *pittam*: bile; *jvaram*: fever; *tṛṣām*: thirst; *ca viṣāṇi*: and poisons.

**Translation**
After drawing in the breath through the tongue, then retaining [it] as before, the wise man should slowly exhale through both nostrils. This breath retention called *śītalī* causes the removal [of] diseases such as *gulma*, *plīha*, bile, fever, thirst and poisons.

**Commentary**
The word *śītalī* means 'cooling' or 'calming'. This kumbhaka cools the body and relaxes the mind. It is performed by breathing in through the rolled tongue, which cools the ingoing breath before it enters the throat and lungs.

***Technique***
Sit in a comfortable meditation position. Close the eyes and

relax the whole body. Allow the breath to become slow and rhythmic. Open the mouth and extend the tongue. Roll the tongue, so that the sides curl upward and inward, forming a tube. The front of the tongue should protrude beyond the lips.

Slowly inhale through the tube-like aperture, formed by the rolled tongue. While inhaling draw the breath and the awareness downward into the chest cavity. At the end of inhalation, withdraw the tongue and close the mouth. Hold the breath inside, relaxing the diaphragm, for a comfortable duration. Exhale slowly through both nostrils. This is one round. Perform ten to twenty rounds, or practice for five to ten minutes.

This breath retention, called śītalī kumbhaka, is very powerful. It removes diseases, such as enlarged spleen and stomach, and other conditions, such as fever, excess bile, hunger, thirst, and poisons.

## Verses 32 to 39: Bhastrika kumbhaka

ततः पद्मासनं बद्ध्वा समग्रीवोदरः सुधीः ।
मुखं संयम्य यत्नेन प्राणं घ्राणेन रेचयेत् ।।३२।।
यथा लगति कण्ठात्तु कपाले सस्वनं ततः ।
वेगेन पूरयेत् किंचिद्धृत्पद्मावधि मारुतम् ।।३३।।
पुनर्विरेचयेत्तद्वत्पूरयेच्च पुनः पुनः ।
यथैव लोहकाराणां भस्त्रा वेगेन चाल्यते ।।३४।।
यथैव स्वशरीरस्थं चालयेत्पवनं शनैः ।
यथा श्रमो भवेद्देह तथा सूर्येण पूरयेत् ।।३५।।
यथोदरं भवेत्पूर्णं पवनेन तथा लघु ।
धारयन्नासिकामध्यं तर्जनीभ्यां विना दृढम् ।।३६।।
कुम्भकं पूर्ववत्कृत्वा रेचयेदिडयानिलम् ।
कण्ठोत्थितानलहरं शरीराग्निविवर्दनम् ।।३७।।
कुण्डलीबोदहकं पुण्यं पापघ्नं शुभदं सुखम् ।
ब्रह्मनाडीमुखान्तस्थकफाद्दर्गलनाशनम् ।।३८।।
गुणत्रयसमुद्भूतग्रन्थित्रयविभेदकम् ।
विशेषेणैव कर्तव्यं भस्त्राख्यं कुम्भकं त्विदम् ।।३९।।

*tataḥ padmāsanaṃ baddhvā samagrīvodaraḥ sudhīḥ*
*mukhaṃ saṃyamya yatnena prāṇaṃ ghrānena recayet* (32)
*yathā lagati kaṇṭhāttu kapāle sasvanaṃ tataḥ*
*vegena pūrayet kiṃciddhṛtpadmāvadhi mārutam* (33)
*punarvirecayettadvatpūrayecca punaḥ punaḥ*
*yathaiva lohakārāṇāṃ bhastrā vegena cālyate* (34)
*yathaiva svaśarīrasthaṃ cālayetpavanaṃ śanaiḥ*
*yathā śramo bhaveddeha tathā sūryeṇa pūrayet* (35)
*yathodaraṃ bhavetpūrṇaṃ pavanena tathā laghu*
*dhārayannāsikāmadhyaṃ tarjanībhyāṃ vinā dṛḍham* (36)
*kumbhakaṃ pūrvavatkṛtvā recayediḍayānilam*

*kaṇṭhotthitānalaharaṃ śarīrāgnivivardanam* (37)
*kuṇḍalībodahakaṃ puṇyaṃ pāpaghnaṃ śubhadaṃ sukham*
*brahmanāḍīmukhāntasthakaphāddargalanāśanam* (38)
*guṇatrayasamudbhūtagranthitrayavibhedakam*
*viśeṣenaiva kartavyaṃ bhastrākhyaṃ kumbhakaṃ tvidam* (39)

**Anvay**

*tataḥ*: then; *baddhvā padmāsanam*: having assumed padmāsana; *grīva*: neck; *udaraḥ*: abdomen; *sama*: upright; *sudhīḥ*: wise man; *mukham*: mouth; *saṃyamya*: closed; *recayet*: should exhale; *yatnena*: with effort; *ghrānena*: through the nose; *yathā lagati*: as soon as this ensues; *pūrayet*: he should draw; *mārutam*: breath; *vegena*: with force; *adhi*: upwards; *padmau*: from the feet; *dhṛt*: holding; *kiṃcit*: a while; *tataḥ*: then; *sasvanam*: loudly; *kaṇṭhāt*: from the neck; *kapāle*: into the skull; *tadvat*: in the same way; *virecayet*: he should exhale; *punaḥ*: again; *ca*: and; *pūrayet*: he should inhale; *punaḥ punaḥ*: again and again; *yatha eva*: just as; *bhastrāḥ*: bellows; *lohakārāṇām*: of blacksmiths; *cālyate*: are moved; *vegena*: with force; *yatha eva*: so; *śanaiḥ*: slowly; *cālayet*: he should move; *pavanam*: air; *svaśarīrastham*: within his own body; *yathā*: if; *deha*: body; *bhavet*: becomes; *śramaḥ*: weary; *tathā*: then; *pūrayet*: he should inhale; *sūryeṇa*: through the right nostril; *yathā*: if; *udaram*: belly; *bhavet*: becomes; *pūrnam*: full; *pavanena*: with air; *tathā*: then; *laghu*: quickly; *dhārayat*: pressing; *madhyam*: centre; *nāsikā*: nostrils; *dṛḍham*: firmly; *vinā tarjanībhyām*: not with the forefingers; *kṛtvā kumbhakam*: retaining the breath; *pūrvavat*: as before; *recayet anilam*: he should exhale; *iḍayā*: through the left nostril; *haram*: destroys; *anala*: bile; *utthita*: rising up; *kaṇṭha*: throat; *vivardanam*: increases; *agni*: digestive fire; *śarīra*: body; *bodhakam*: arouses; *kuṇḍalī*: kuṇḍalinī; *puṇyam*: purifies; *pāpaghnam*: destroying sins; *śubhadam*: gives auspiciousness; *sukham*: happiness; *nāśanam*: destroys; *argala*: bolt; *ādi*: beginning; *kapha*: phlegm; *antastha*: is at the end; *mukha*: mouth; *brahmanāḍī*: *brahmanāḍī*; *vibhedakam*: it pierces; *granthi-traya*: three *granthis*, knots; *samudbhūta*: produced by; *guṇa-traya*: three *guṇas*, characteristics; *idam kumbhakam*: this kumbhaka; *ākhyam*: called; *bhastrā*: bellows [breath]; *viśeṣena*: especially; *kartavyam*: should be performed.

**Translation**

Then, the wise man having assumed padmāsana, neck and abdomen upright, mouth closed, should exhale with effort through the nose. As soon as this ensues, he should draw the breath with force upwards from the feet, then loudly from the neck into the skull, holding [it] a while. In the same way he should exhale again, and inhale again and again. Just as the bellows of blacksmiths are moved with force, so he should slowly move the air within his own body. If the body becomes weary, then he should inhale through the right nostril. If the belly becomes full of air, then quickly pressing the centre [of] the nostrils firmly [but] not with the forefingers, [and] retaining the breath as before, he should exhale through the left nostril.

[This kumbhaka] destroys the bile rising up the throat, increases the digestive fire [of] the body, arouses kuṇḍalinī, purifies [by] destroying sins, gives auspiciousness [and] happiness, [and] destroys the bolt [of] the beginning [of] phlegm [which] is at the end [of] the mouth [of] *brahmanāḍī*. It pierces the three *granthis* produced by the three *guṇas*. This kumbhaka, called bellows [breath], should be especially performed.

**Commentary**

The word *bhastrika* comes from the root *bhastra*, meaning 'bellows'. Hence, it is known as the bellows breathing. Just as the blacksmith of old fanned the fire of his trade with the bellows, this kumbhaka fans the yogic fire within the abdomen. Bhastrika is a dynamic prāṇāyāma, which utilises forceful breathing to draw air in and out of the lungs. In this way, it activates the maṇipura cakra, located behind the navel, and increases the internal heat. Regular practice of bhastrika is an important method of purification, because it burns up all the impurities accumulated in the body, whether physical, pranic or mental.

***Technique***

Sit in padmāsana, the lotus posture, or in any comfortable meditation position. Ensure that the head, neck and spine are upright. Relax the whole body from head to toe. Close the mouth and breath through the nose.

Exhale forcefully through the nose. At the end of exhalation, draw the breath in with force, mentally directing it upward through the body from the feet to the chest, and then loudly from the neck into the head. Hold the breath for a few moments, focusing at ajña cakra at the mid brain, and then exhale forcefully through the nose.

Go on exhaling and inhaling forcefully in the same way, again and again. Move the air through your own body, just as the blacksmith fans the fire forcefully with his bellows.

If the body becomes tired, close the left nostril, pressing it with the middle finger, and inhale forcefully through the right nostril. If the abdomen fills with air, press the center of both nostrils firmly with the middle finger and the thumb at the end of inhalation. Retain the breath as before, and then exhale through the left nostril.

Bhastrika kumbhaka has many benefits. It increases the digestive fire and improves the entire digestive process, preventing regurgitation of bile and acid in the throat. It arouses the kuṇḍalinī śakti and removes the bolt of phlegm at the mouth of *brahmanāḍī*, the innermost channel of suṣumnā, allowing the kuṇḍalinī force to arise unimpeded. It purifies the entire system, destroys negative propensities, and bestows auspiciousness and happiness upon the practitioner.

This kumbhaka pierces the three *granthis*, or psychic knots, which bind us into the material dimension by inhibiting our spiritual evolution. These three knots include: *brahma* granthi, the knot of procreation, *viṣṇu* granthi, the knot of sustaining and loving life, and *rudra* granthi, the knot of fearing dissolution. These three granthis, which affect all who are born, are the product of the three *guṇas,* or qualities of nature: *sattwa* (balance), *rajas* (dynamism) and *tamas* (stability). For these reasons, the above verses recommend that bhastrika kumbhaka should be especially performed.

## Verses 40 and 41: Three bandhas

चतुर्णामपि भेदानां कुम्भके समुपस्थिते ।
बन्धत्रयमिदं कार्यं योगिभिर्वीतकल्मशैः ।।४०।।
प्रथमो मूलबन्धस्तु द्वितीयोड्डीयणाभिधः ।
जालन्धरस्तृतीयस्तु तेषां लक्षणमुच्यते ।।४१।।

*caturṇāmapi bhedānāṃ kumbhake samupasthite*
*bandhatrayamidaṃ kāryaṃ yogibhirvītakalmaśaiḥ* (40)
*prathamo mūlabandhastu dvitīyoḍḍīyaṇābhidhaḥ*
*jālandharastṛtīyastu teṣāṃ lakṣaṇamucyate* (41)

**Anvay**
*caturṇām api bhedānām*: through those four means; *kumbhake samupasthite*: when kumbhaka is imminent; *idam bandha-trayam*: these three bandhas; *kāryam*: should be performed; *yogibhiḥ*: by the yogins; *vītakalmaśaiḥ*: who are untainted; *prathamaḥ*: first; *mūlabandhaḥ*: perineal lock; *dvitīya*: second; *ābhidhaḥ*: is called; *uḍḍīyana*: abdominal lock; *tu*: and; *tṛtīyaḥ*: third; *jālandhara*: throat lock; *lakṣaṇam*: detailed description; *teṣām*: of them; *ucyate*: is given.

**Translation**
Through those four means, when kumbhaka is imminent, these three bandhas should be performed by the yogins, who are untainted. The first [is] *mūlabandha*; the second is called *uḍḍīyana* and the third *jālandhara.* A detailed description of them is given [here].

**Commentary**
The 'four means'referred to above are the four prāṇāyāmas: sūryabheda, ujjāyī, śitalī and bhastrika. While performing these practices, at the time of kumbhaka, the three *bandhas*, or psychic locks, should be applied. The bandhas have a powerful effect on the prāṇas, nāḍīs and cakras. Therefore, one should undergo purification through diet, lifestyle and

practice, before utilising them. The bandhas should be applied while performing kumbhaka in the following order: first, mūlabandha, the perineal lock; second, uḍḍīyana bandha, the abdominal lock, and third, jālandhara, the throat lock. Although it is recommended here to apply the three bandhas during kumbhaka, it is very important to establish them first, by practising one bandha at a time. A detailed description of each bandha is given in the following verses.

## Verses 42 to 46: Mūlabandha

अधोगतिमपानं वै ऊर्ध्वगं कुरुते बलात् ।
आकुञ्चनेन तं प्रहुर्मूलबन्धोऽयमुच्यते ।।४२।।
अपाने चोर्ध्वगे याते संप्राप्ते वह्निमण्डले ।
ततो ऽनलशिखा दीर्घा वर्धते वायुनाहता ।।४३।।
ततो यातौ वह्न्यपानौ प्राणमुष्णस्वरूपकम् ।
तेनात्यन्तप्रदीप्तेन ज्वलनो देहजस्तथा ।।४४।।
तेन कुण्डलिनी सुप्ता संतप्ता संप्रबुध्यते ।
दण्डाहतभुजङ्गेव निःश्वस्य ऋजुतां व्रजेत् ।।४५।।
बिलप्रवेशितो यत्र ब्रह्मनाड्यन्तरं व्रजेत् ।
तस्मान्नित्यं मूलबन्धः कर्तव्यो योगिभिः सदा ।।४६।।

*adhogatimapānaṃ vai ūrdhvagaṃ kurute balāt*
*ākuñcanena taṃ prahurmūlabandho 'yamucyate* (42)
*apāne cordhvage yāte saṃprāpte vahnimaṇḍale*
*tato 'nalaśikhā dīrghā vardhate vāyunāhatā* (43)
*tato yātau vahnyapānau prāṇamuṣṇasvarūpakam*
*tenātyantapradīptena jvalano dehajastathā* (44)
*tena kuṇḍalinī suptā saṃtaptā saṃprabudhyate*
*daṇḍāhatabhujaṅgeva niḥśvasya ṛjutāṃ vrajet* (45)
*bilapraveśito yatra brahmanāḍyantaraṃ vrajet*
*tasmānnityaṃ mūlabandhaḥ kartavyo yogibhiḥ sadā* (46)

**Anvay**

*apāna*: one of the five pranas, flowing in-between the waist and the pelvic floor; *adhogatim*: downward movement; *balāt*: forcibly; *kurute*: is made; *ūrdhvagam*: go upwards; *ākuñcanena*: by bending forward; *ayam prahuḥ*: this offering; *ucyate*: is called; *mūlabandhaḥ*: perineal lock; *ca*: and; *apāne yāte ūrdhvage*: when *apāna* goes upwards; *samprāpte*: arriving at; *maṇḍale*: sphere; *vahni*: agni; *tataḥ*: then; *śikhā*: flame; *anala*: agni; *vardhate*: grows; *dīrghā*: long; *vāyunā-*

*āhatā*: buffeted by *vāyu*; *tataḥ*: then; *vahni-apānau*: agni and apāna; *svarūpakam*: in the form; *uṣṇa*: heat; *yātau*: enter; *prāṇam*:one of the five pranas, flowing sideways from the diaphragm to the waist; *tenāt*: through this; *atyanta*: powerfully; *pradīptena*: blazing; *jvalanaḥ*: fire; *tathā*: thus; *deha-jaḥ*: is produced in the body; *tena*: so; *suptā kuṇḍalinī*: sleeping kuṇḍalinī; *saṃprabudhyate*: is awakened; *saṃtaptā*: glowing heat; *niḥśvasya*: hissing; *vrajet*: becomes; *ṛjutām*: erect; *iva*: like; *bhujanga*: snake; *āhata*: struck; *daṇḍa*: stick; *praveśitaḥ*: it enters; *bila*: opening; *brahmanāḍī*: subtlest channel within the sushumna; *vrajet*: moving; *antaram yatra*: inside there; *tasmāt*: therefore; *mūlabandhaḥ*: perineal lock; *sadā*: always; *kartavyaḥ*: should be practised; *nityam*: daily; *yogibhiḥ*: by the yogins.

**Translation**

*Apāna,* [which has] a downward movement, is forcibly made [to] go upwards by bending forward. This offering is called *mūlabandha*. And when *apāna* goes upwards, arriving at the sphere [of] agni, then the flame [of] agni grows long, buffeted by *vāyu*. Then agni and apāna, in the form [of] heat, enter prāṇa. Through this [process], a powerfully blazing fire is thus produced in the body, [and] so the sleeping kuṇḍalinī is awakened [by] its glowing heat. [Then the kuṇḍalinī], hissing, becomes erect like a snake struck [by] a stick. It enters the opening [of] *brahmanāḍi,* moving inside there. Therefore, mūlabandha should always be practised daily by the yogins.

**Commentary**

Mūlabandha, the perineal lock, is an important practice for the awakening of kuṇḍalinī. It is said that the kuṇḍalinī force lies in a dormant state at the mūlādhāra cakra until it is awakened. Normally, apāna prāṇa flows downward in the body from the waist to the pelvic floor. This downward flowof energy is responsible for the elimination processes, such as urination, defecation, expulsion of gas and wind, reproductive fluids and even the fetus at the time of birth. In this process, the downward flow of energy is generally lost as the waste products leave the body. However, by applying mūlabandha, the downward flow of apāna is reversed and directed upward. This reversal of the downward flow of apāna by the application of mūlabandha activates mūlādhāra cakra and awakens the kuṇḍalinī force.

***Technique***

Sit in siddhāsana or any other comfortable meditation āsana. Allow the body to become calm and still. Become aware of the natural breath, flowing in and out.

Inhale slowly and deeply through both nostrils. At the end of inhalation, hold the breath inside and bend forward slightly. Pulling upward with the muscles of the pelvic floor, contract the perineum, mid-way between the urinary organ and the anal sphincter. In females, the contraction should take place in the upper vagina, where it meets the cervix.

Hold the contraction and the breath for a few moments. Experience the combined kumbhaka with contraction, reversing the downward flow of apāna energy. Continue holding the contraction and the breath, and feel the energy rising from the pelvic floor, upward into the sphere of *agni*, or fire, located behind the navel.

With the merging of apāna into the circle of agni, behind the navel, the flame of fire becomes long, extending upward towards the sphere of *vāyu*, or air, in the region of the heart. Feel the flame, being fanned by vāyu, grows hotter and stronger.

Now, agni and apāna, in the form of heat, enter the field of prāna at the maṇipura cakra, the psychic center behind the navel in suṣumnā. This process produces a powerful, blazing fire in the body, which is known as the yogic fire.

The sleeping kuṇḍalinī is awakened by the glowing heat of

this fire. Hissing, the kuṇḍalinī uncoils herself and becomes erect. Then, she enters the opening of *brahmanāḍī*, the subtlemost channel of suṣumnā, and arises inside from there.

Hence, mūlabandha is a major method of kuṇḍalinī yoga, and should be practised daily by the yogins.

### Verses 47 to 50: Uḍḍīyana bandha

कुम्भकान्ते रेचकादौ कर्तव्यस्तूड्डियाणकः ।
बन्धो येन सुषुम्नायां प्राणस्तूड्डीयते यतः ।।४७।।
तस्मादुड्डीयणाख्योऽयं योगिभिः समुदाहृतः ।
सति वज्रासने पादौ कराभ्या धारयेद्द्वढम् ।।४८।।
गुल्फदेशसमीपे च कन्दं तत्र प्रपीडेत् ।
पश्चिमं ताणमुदरे धारयेद्धृदये गले ।।४९।।
शनैः शनैर्यदा प्राणस्तुन्दसन्धिं निगच्छति ।
तुन्ददोषं विनिर्धूय कर्तव्यं सततं शनैः ।।५०।।

*kumbhakānte recakādau kartavyastūḍḍiyāṇakaḥ*
*bandho yena suṣumnāyāṃ prāṇastūḍḍīyate yataḥ* (47)
*tasmāduḍḍīyaṇākhyo 'yaṃ yogibhiḥ samudāhṛtaḥ*
*sati vajrāsane pādau karābhyā dhārayeddvaḍham* (48)
*gulphadeśasamīpe ca kandaṃ tatra prapīḍet*
*paścimaṃ tāṇamudare dhārayeddhṛdaye gale* (49)
*śanaiḥ śanairyadā prāṇastundasandhiṃ nigacchati*
*tundadoṣaṃ vinirdhūya kartavyaṃ satataṃ śanaiḥ* (50)

**Anvay**

*tu*: now; *ūḍḍiyāṇakaḥ*: abdominal lock; *kartavyaḥ*: should be performed; *kumbhaka-anta*: at the end of kumbhaka; *recaka-ādau*: at the beginning of exhalation; *yataḥ*: because; *yena*: through this; *prāṇa uḍḍīyate*: flies up; *suṣumnāyām*: suṣumnā; *ayam bandhaḥ*: this bandha; *tasmāt*: therefore; *samudāhṛtaḥ*: is called; *uḍḍīyaṇa*: *uḍḍīyaṇa*; *yogibhiḥ*: by yogins; *sati*: remaining; *vajrāsane*: in *vajrāsana*; *dhārayet*: one should grasp; *dvaḍham*: both; *pādau*: feet; *karābhyā*: with both hands; *ca*: and; *prapīḍet*: one should press; *tatra*: there; *kandam*: *kanda*; *deśa*: place; *samīpe*: near; *gulpha*: ankles; *dhārayet*: one should hold; *śanaiḥ śanaiḥ*: very slowly; *paścimam*: back side; *tānam*: thread, nāḍī; *udare*: in the abdomen; *hṛdaye*: in the heart; *gale*: in the throat; *yadā*:

when; *prāṇah*: prāṇa; *nigacchati*: reaches; *sandhim*: junction; *tunda*: navel; *vinirdhūya*: it drives away; *doṣam*: disease; *tunda*: navel; *kartavyam*: should be done; *satatam*: regularly.

**Translation**

Now *uḍḍīyaṇa* should be performed at the end of kumbhaka [and] the beginning of exhalation. Because through this [practice] prāṇa flies up suṣumnā, this bandha is therefore called *uḍḍīyaṇa* by yogins. Remaining in *vajrāsana*, one should firmly grasp the feet with both hands, and press there the *kanda* [at] the place near the ankles. One should very slowly hold the [awareness] at the back side [of] the thread or nāḍī in the abdomen, heart [and] throat. When prāṇa reaches the junction [of] the navel, it drives away disease [in] the navel. [So the practice] should be done regularly.

**Commentary**

Uḍḍīyana bandha, the abdominal lock, is another important practice of kuṇḍalinī yoga. The word *uḍḍīyana* comes from the root *ud*, meaning 'to raise up' or 'to fly upward'. This abdominal contraction activates the kuṇḍalinī and directs it upward on its ascent through the brahmanāḍī, within the suṣumnā. The above verse says that uḍḍīyana should be initiated at the end of internal kumbhaka, and the beginning of exhalation. This description of uḍḍīyana bandha is different to the practice, as it is taught today, and is not found in other classical yoga texts, although the result of the practice is the same, ie. the prāṇa flies upward through suṣumnā.

The above verse recommends uḍḍīyana bandha to be performed, while sitting in the posture of vajrāsana. Refer to the explanation given for vajrāsana in the previous verses (4-6) for clarification on this position. Vajrāsana was earlier known as muktāsana, or guptāsana, both being different names for the posture of siddhāsana. The technique further mentions the *kanda*, which is the root of the nāḍīs, situated in the pelvic region, in-between the navel and the anus. Activation of the kanda causes the kuṇḍalinī to arise.

***Technique***

Sit quietly in siddhāsana and relax the entire body from head to toe. Allow the body to become steady and still. Become aware of the natural breath flowing in and out through the nostrils.

Breathe in slowly and deeply. Hold the breath inside for a comfortable duration. Towards the end of internal retention, just before exhalation, firmly grasp the feet with both hands, and press the *kanda* in-between the ankles and the navel.

Exhaling slowly, rotate the prāṇa upward through suṣumnā, the thread behind, to the abdomen, heart and throat. At the end of exhalation, bring the prāṇa and the awareness straight back to the navel.

Hold the breath outside and contract the abdomen, pulling the navel inward towards the back and then drawing it upward. Hold the contraction and the external retention for as long as you feel comfortable.

When the external retention is complete, release the abdominal contraction and the hold on the ankles. Relax and allow the breath to normalise before beginning the next round.

When the prāṇa is activated at the navel by this lock, it triggers manipura chakra and the storehouse of prāṇa situated there. This energy boosts the entire system and regulates the digestive organs, removing disease in the abdominal region. Yogis often suffer from digestive ailments due to the introverted sādhanas they perform. Therefore, this practice should be done by them regularly.

## Verses 51 to 55: Jālandhara bandha

पूरकान्ते तु कर्तव्यो बन्धो जालन्धराभिधः ।
कण्ठसंकोचरूपोऽसौ वायुमार्गनिरोधकः ।।५१।।
अधस्तात्कुञ्चनेनाशु कण्ठसंकोचने कृते ।
मध्ये पश्चिमताणेन स्यात्प्राणो ब्रह्मनाडिगः ।।५२।।
पूर्वोक्तेन क्रमेणैव सम्यगासनमास्थितः
चालनं तु सरस्वत्याः कृत्वा प्राणं निरोधयेत् ।।५३।।
प्रथमे दिवसे कार्यं कुम्भकानां चुतष्यम् ।
प्रत्येकं दशसंख्याकं द्वितीये पञ्चभिस्तथा ।।५४।।
विंशत्यलं तृतीयेऽह्नि पञ्चवृद्ध्या दिनेदिने ।
कर्तव्यः कुम्भको नित्यं बन्धत्रयसमन्वितः ।।५५।।

*pūrakānte tu kartavyo bandho jālandharābhidhaḥ*
*kaṇṭhasaṃkocarūpo 'sau vāyumārganirodhakaḥ* (51)
*adhastātkuñcanenāśu kaṇṭhasaṃkocane kṛte*
*madhye paścimatāṇena syātprāṇo brahmanāḍigaḥ* (52)
*pūrvoktena krameṇaiva samyagāsanamāsthitaḥ*
*cālanaṃ tu sarasvatyāḥ kṛtvā prāṇaṃ nirodhayet* (53)
*prathame divase kāryaṃ kumbhakānāṃ cutaṣyam*
*pratyekaṃ daśasaṃkhyākaṃ dvitīye pañcabhistathā* (54)
*viṃśatyalaṃ tṛtīye 'hni pañcavṛddhyā dinedine*
*kartavyaḥ kumbhako nityaṃ bandhatrayasamanvitaḥ* (55)

**Anvay**

*tu*: now; *bandhaḥ*: bandha, lock; *abhidhaḥ*: of the name; *jālandhara*: jālandhara; *kartavyaḥ*: is to be done; *pūrakānte*: at the end of inhalation; *asau*: this; *rūpaḥ*: form; *saṃkoca*: contraction; *kaṇṭha*: throat; *nirodhakaḥ*: obstructing; *vāyu-mārga*: path of vāyu; *kaṇṭha-saṃkocane kṛte*: when the throat is contracted; *āśu*: quickly; *kuñcnena*: by bending; *adhastāt*: down; *prāṇaḥ*: prāṇa; *syāt*: is; *paścima-tāṇena*: on the western thread; *madhye*: in the middle; *brahmanāḍi-gaḥ*: on its way through brahmanāḍī; *āsthitaḥ*: staying in; *samyak āsanam*: same posture; *pūrvoktena*: as before; *tu*: and; *cālanam kṛtvā*: stirring up; *sarasvatyāḥ*: saraswatī; *krameṇa*: gradually; *nirodhayet*: one controls; *prāṇam*: prāṇa; *prathame divase*: on the first day; *catuḥ*: four; *kāryam*: should be done; *dvitīye*: on the second; *daśa-saṃkhyākam*: ten times; *tathā*: then; *pañcabhiḥ*: five; *pratyekam*: singly; *tṛtīye ahni*: on the third day; *viṃśati-alam*: twenty times; *kumbhakaḥ kartavyaḥ*: kumbhaka should be practised; *nityam*: always; *samanvitaḥ*: together with; *bandha-traya*: three bandhas; *pañca-vṛddhyā*: with an increase of five; *dinedine*: each day.

**Translation**

Now the bandha of the name jālandhara is to be done at the end of inhalation. This [bandha is of] the form [of] contraction [of] the throat, obstructing the path of vāyu. When the throat is contracted by quickly bending down, the prāṇa is on the western thread in the middle on its way through brahmanāḍī. Staying in the same posture as before and stirring up saraswatī, one gradually controls the prāṇa. On the first day, four [rounds] of kumbhaka should be done, on the second [day], ten times, then five singly, [and] on the third day twenty times. Kumbhaka should always be practised together with the three bandhas [and] with an increase of five [rounds] each day.

**Commentary**

Jālandhara bandha is the throat lock. The word *jālan* means 'net' and the word *dhara*, 'stream' or 'flow'. Hence, the flow of prāṇa and consciousness is netted and locked at the throat by this bandha. The practice of bandha is ancient and relates to the tantric concept of *amrit*, or immortal nectar, the energy of life that drips downward continually from the moon at *bindu visarga,* the point at the top back of the head. This flow of nectar is a higher form of energy, responsible for the prāṇa and consciousness, which maintain the life of the individual.

If this energy can be retained in the region of the head, it heightens perception of the subtle dimensions of knowledge and existence. If it is allowed to fall down into the body, however, it is used up by the physical processes, which leads to degeneration, old age and ultimately death.

Yogis of old, therefore, practised jālandhara bandha in order to net this energy of life and redirect it back to the higher regions in the head. When this energy falls down into the body, it first passes through *viśuddhi cakra*, at the throat region, where it gets spent in speech and and emotional expression. From there, it passes down to *maṇipura cakra*, behind the navel, where it is consumed by the metabolic and digestive fire, as well as the activities in the external world. The remaining energy falls down to the lower cakras, *mūlādhāra* and *swādhisthana*, where it is transformed into *ojas* or sexual energy, and discharged through sexual attraction and interaction.

This pathway of the descent of life energy was well understood by the yogis of old, and they used the three bandhas to redirect this subtle force back up to the higher centers in the head. When the energy fell down to the throat region, it was redirected upward by jālandhara bandha. When it fell down further into the abdominal region, it was rechannelled by uḍḍiyāna bandha. And when it fell into the lower centres, the flow was reversed by mūla bandha. Although, the three bandhas should be mastered separately, later on, all three can be performed together. Then the practice is called *maha bandha,* the great lock.

***Technique***

Sit in siddhāsana, or any comfortable meditation posture. Place the hands on the knees with the palms facing downward. Relax the whole body, and allow it to become steady and still. Become aware of the natural breath. Focus on the breath, flowing in and out at the nose tip. Feel the breath becoming slow and even.

Bring the awareness down to the pelvic floor, and direct the flow of inhalation up the *brahmanāḍī*, at the center of suṣumnā, from mūlādhāra cakra at the base to ajña cakra at the mid-brain. Exhale back down from ajña to mūlādhāra, directing the flow of breath through the brahmanāḍī. Continue the rotation of breath and awareness up and down, stirring up the energy in suṣumnā.

Next, at the end of inhalation, when the breath reaches viśuddhi cakra behind the throat, quickly bend the head forward, so that the chin touches the chest. Hold the breath inside. Straighten the arms and press downward with the hands on the knees. Hold the breath retention and the throat lock for as long as you feel comfortable. Then bend the elbows, raise the head, and exhale slowly back down the brahmanāḍī to mūlādhāra cakra at the base.

Allow the breath to normalise, and then begin the next round. At first, four rounds of jālandhara kumbhaka can be done. Gradually increase the practice to ten rounds. Then do five rounds of each bandha: mūla bandha, uḍḍiyāna bandha and jālandhara bandha, one by one.

Finally, practise maha bandha at the end of exhalation, combining the three bandhas, one after the other, for five rounds. Remain in the same posture, and go on stirring up the energy in suṣumnā, gradually gaining control over the prāṇa. Increase the practice when you feel ready, five rounds at a time, up to twenty rounds.

## Verses 56 to 58: First obstacle to yoga

दिवा सुप्तिर्निशायां तु जागरादतिमैथुनात् ।
बहुसंक्रमणं नित्यं रोधान्मूत्रपुरीषयोः ।।५६।।
विषमाशनदोषाच्च प्रयासप्राणचिन्तनात् ।
शीघ्रमुत्पद्यते रोगः स्तम्भयेद्यदि संयमी ।।५७।।
योगाभ्यासेन मे रोग उत्पन्न इति कथ्यते ।
ततोऽभ्यासं त्यजेदेवं प्रथमं विघ्नोच्यते ।।५८।।

*divā suptirniśāyāṃ tu jāgarādatimaithunāt*
*bahusaṃkramaṇaṃ nityaṃ rodhānmūtrapurīṣayoḥ* (56)
*viṣamāśanadoṣācca prayāsaprāṇacintanāt*
*śīghramutpadyate rogaḥ stambhayedyadi samyamī* (57)
*yogābhyāsena me roga utpanna iti kathyate*
*tato 'bhyāsaṃ tyajedevaṃ prathamaṃ vighnocyate* (58)

**Anvay**

*rogaḥ*: disease; *śīghram*: quickly; *utpadyate*: is caused; *suptiḥ*: by sleeping; *divā*: during the day; *jāgarāt-ati*: by staying awake late; *niśāyām*: at night; *bahu maithunāt*: by too much sexual intercourse; *nityam saṃkramaṇam*: continual socialising; *rodhān*: obstructions; *mūtra-purīṣayoḥ*: urine [and] faeces; *doṣāt*: by the bad habit; *viṣamāśana*: irregular eating; *ca*: and; *prāṇa*: energy; *cintanāt prayāsa*: through mental exertion; *yadi*: if; *samyamī*: yogin; *stambhayet*: stops; *iti kathyate*: saying; *me rogaḥ*: my disease; *utpannaḥ*: has appeared; *yoga-abhyāsena*: through the practice of yoga; *tataḥ*: then; *tyajet*: he gives up; *abhyāsam*: practice; *evam ucyate*: this is said; *prathamam vighna*: first obstacle.

**Translation**

Disease is quickly caused by sleeping during the day, staying awake late at night, too much sexual intercourse, continual socialising, obstructions [of] urine [and] faeces, bad habit [of] irregular eating and [too much] energy through mental exertion. If the yogin stops [the practice], saying 'My disease has appeared through the practice of yoga', then he gives up his practice. This is said [to be] the first obstacle [to yoga].

**Commentary**

The above verses explain very simply the causes of disease, which have all become a way of life in our time. The first causes given are: irregular sleeping hours, sleeping during the day and staying awake late at night. The natural sleep cycle should be about eight hours per night, and in rhythm with the sun. The sun rises around six am and sets around six pm, with seasonal variations and also depending on location. However, in the modern world, many people prefer to stay up past midnight and then get up much later. Traditionally, the best time for yoga and meditation is at dawn, in-between four and six am. This is a special time, known as *brahma muhurta*, when the environment is very pure and still. Similarly, in the evening, the best time is at dusk, in-between four and six pm. These two times of the day also relate with an increased flow of *sushumna*, which is very helpful for achieving inner experience.

However, it is not possible for a person to practice regularly at dawn and at dusk, without first regulating the sleep patterns. As long as one is in the habit of sleeping late, one will arise late, because a certain amount of sleep is needed each night. Adequate sleep is essential for the health and balance of the entire system. In modern life, where the entire society goes to sleep late, it becomes difficult to sleep earlier. The vibrations all around do not support silence, introversion and rest. If one sleeps late and gets up early, sleep deprivation arises, which can lead to chronic stress and low energy. In order to get the proper amount of sleep, one sleeps during the day. This imbalanced sleep cycle becomes a habit and causes disease over time.

The second cause of disease is excessive sexual activity.

Sexual emissions are not waste products. They are a vital form of energy, known as *ojas*, which has the possibility to create new life. When this energy is overused, it depletes the nervous system and the prana. Excessive sexual drive is counter-productive for yogis, and causes weakness and disease in the society. This is why *brahmacārya*, or sexual abstention, was practised by the yogis of old. Nowadays, moderation in sexual activity is recommended. One may also consider the energy exchange that takes place with each sexual interaction. This is why it is recommended in yoga to engage with one partner, rather than with many. For a person, who is addicted to sexuality with many partners, progress in yoga becomes remote, and disease draws near.

The number three cause of disease is continual socialising. This is very interesting, because in modern life, socialising is regarded as healthy. The more one socialises, the better integrated and accepted one is. Many people keep appointment books with meetings at every possible hour of the day. They feel that unless this book is filled, their lives are not meaningful. The yogi, on the other hand, regards socialising as a necessary evil, and only complies when absolutely necessary. This is because constant socialising extroverts the mind and keeps it on high alert. Even when one has a quiet moment, thoughts of previous conversations and interactions fill the mind with unease, stress and fruitless expectations. The need for continual socialising causes an energetic imbalance, which develops from a young age, and becomes a cause of disease, as we get older, without our even realising it.

The number four cause of disease is obstruction of urine and faeces. Urinary blockage may be caused by urinary tract infection or disease, or stones in the kidney or urinary tract. In later years, men may suffer urinary blockage due to enlarged prostate gland. Constipation, or difficulty in eliminating faeces, has many causes, such as: busy and stressful lifestyle, fast food, dry and hard food from packets, dehydration, and inadequate exercise. Obstruction of elimination is the mother of all diseases, and leads to chronic energy imbalance, toxicity and dullness. The yogic practitioner, who suffers from this condition, will need to adjust the diet, lifestyle and yoga practice accordingly, so that these problems are eliminated.

The number five cause of disease is irregularity in eating and poor food choices. In order to progress in yoga, the diet and lifestyle must be regulated and sattvic. The food one choses to eat on a daily basis should be light, pure and fresh. Instead of combining many food items, meals should be simple, consisting of two or three items. Food should be well cooked, but not overcooked, with a minimum of raw food. Meal timings should be planned around the movement of the sun, which relates with the digestive fire in the body. So, just after sunrise, a small meal can be taken. When the sun is at its zenith, around noon, a large meal can be assimilated. Later on, just after sunset, a small meal can be consumed. By following these dietary guidelines, the yogic practitioner avoids many diseases.

The number six cause of disease is excessive mental exertion, which is also a symptom of modern life. Many of us are mentally active all day and into the night. Although we may try to get some physical exercise, the mental activity far exceeds the physical. This creates a basic and chronic energetic imbalance, which may be at the root of many diseases that people suffer today. When we use the mind in a focused way, such as study, research and contemplation, mental energy is utilised. When the mind is used in an unfocused way, such as entertainment, socialising, day dreaming, fantasising, mental energy is dissipated. Mental energy is more subtle and powerful than physical energy, and it easily becomes discharged, like a battery. When the mind runs on low energy, it becomes flat and stress levels rise.

This is another major cause of disease.

When the yogi believes that disease has arisen due to the practice of yoga, rather than to the actual causes referred to above, he or she faces the first obstruction to yoga. This obstacle is very difficult to overcome, and arises at some point during the sādhana for most practitioners, because everyone born in the body is susceptible to disease. When this obstruction arises, the yogi should recognise the real causes of disease, and work to eliminate them. In this way, the yoga practice may be temporarily adjusted to suit the condition, and then resumed more seriously, when the disease passes. However, if one blames yoga for the disease, his/her practice will be given up and perhaps never resumed. The most valuable asset of the yogi is the practice. He or she must be determined to maintain it, even in the most difficult situations, such as loss of health and welfare. The practice may be reduced; it may be hidden, but it should never be blamed as the cause of disease and given up.

## Verses 59 to 61: Following nine obstacles

द्वितीय संशयाख्यं च तृतीयं च प्रमत्तता ।
आलस्याख्यं चतुर्थं च निद्रारूपं तु पञ्चमम् ।।५९।।
षष्ठं तु विरतिर्भ्रान्तिः सप्तमं परिकीर्तितम् ।
विषमं चाष्टमं चैव अनास्था नवमं स्मृतम् ।।६०।।
अलब्धिर्योगतत्त्वस्य दशमं प्रोच्यते बुधैः ।
इत्येतद्विघ्नदशकं विचारेण त्यजेद्बुधः ।।६१।।

*dvitīya saṃśayākhyaṃ ca tṛtīyaṃ ca pramattatā*
*ālasyākhyaṃ caturthaṃ ca nidrārūpaṃ tu pañcamam* (59)
*ṣaṣṭhaṃ tu viratirbhrāntiḥ saptamaṃ parikīrtitam*
*viṣamaṃ cāṣṭamaṃ caiva anāsthā navamaṃ smṛtam* (60)
*alabdhiryogatattvasya daśamaṃ procyate budhaiḥ*
*ityetadvighnadaśakaṃ vicāreṇa tyajedbudhaḥ* (61)

**Anvay**

*dvitīya*: second; *ākhyam*: is called; *saṃśaya*: doubt; *tṛtīyam*: third; *pramattatā*: inattentiveness; *caturtham*: fourth; *ālasya*: laziness; *pañcamam*: fifth; *nidrārūpam*: sleep; *ṣaṣṭham*: sixth; *viratiḥ*: erratic; *saptamam*: seventh; *bhrāntiḥ*: confusion; *aṣṭamam*: eighth; *viṣamam*: distress; *navamam*: ninth; *anāsthā*: lack of faith; *ca*: and; *daśamam*: tenth; *procyate*: is called; *budhaiḥ*: by the wise; *alabdhiḥ*: inability to attain; *yoga-tattvasya*: essence of yoga; *iti*: thus; *vicāreṇa*: after reflecting; *budhaḥ*: wise one; *tyajet*: should forgo; *etat daśakam vighna*: these ten obstacles.

**Translation**

The second is called doubt, the third inattentiveness, the fourth laziness, the fifth sleep, the sixth erratic [practice], the seventh confusion, the eighth distress, the ninth lack of faith, and the tenth is called by the wise the inability to attain the essence of yoga. Thus, after reflecting [on these], the wise one should forgo these ten obstacles.

**Commentary**

The serious practitioner of yoga needs to understand and recognise the obstructions that may arise during the period of sādhana. In the earlier teaching, the sādhana given here is prāṇāyāma and bandha. However, the same obstructions may arise in the course of other sādhanas as well. The above verses enumerate the following nine obstructions: (ii) doubt, (iii) inattentiveness, (iv) laziness, (v) sleep, (vi) irregular practice, (vii) confusion, (viii) distress, (ix) lack of faith, and (x) inability to attain the subtle states of yoga.

***Doubt*** is the second obstruction to sadhana, because it becomes an obsession and weakens the resolve to practice. Doubt may arise for many reasons, for example: we are unsure that the practice is correct or the best one for us. We feel there may be another better practice, or a different system, which will help us attain our goals more easily or quickly. We begin to doubt the teacher and the teaching related with the practice, and start to look around for other teachers, systems and techniques. This obstruction is probably more difficult to overcome today, than it was in the past, because there is so much intellectualisation, and there are so many teachers and teachings. Yoga practice does not yield instantaneous results; it needs to be continued assiduously, over a long period of time. This requires commitment and dedication. As soon as doubt arises, one must have the willpower to dispel it. Otherwise, one will leave the practice in search of another and then another.

With each new practice, the will and the commitment to continue grow weaker, until the practice can no longer be sustained. We have all heard the story about the man, who needed water for his crops, and decided to dig a well. A douser recommended a good place to find water, and the man began to dig. In a few days he had dug down about 30 feet, but still he found no water. So, he gave up on that place, and decided to choose another. In the second place that was selected, he dug down about 25 feet, and then began to think that there would be no water there either. So, he climbed out of the second well, and went in search of another location. The man continued in this way, and after several months he had dug about 50 wells, but he never did find any water. This is the story of many yoga practitioners. Therefore, doubt needs to be managed, if one is to progress in the practice. Doubt is easily managed by one who has already attained some spiritual experience. In the absence of experience, however, one must rely on positive associations, study of spiritual teachings and biographies, and firm resolution.

***Inattentiveness*** is the third obstruction, which reduces our ability to succeed at anything, whether inner work or outer work. When we say that our concentration is poor, we really mean our ability to remain attentive is weak. We develop the habit of inattention from an early age. As soon as our interest in some person, someplace or something wanes, we become inattentive. All activities require a certain degree of attention, whether mental or physical, and yoga is no different. In fact, the actual purpose of yoga and meditation is really to develop and direct our attention, to become attentive at will, and remain attentive for longer periods of time. The only difference is the object and plane of attention. With family, social or professional engagements, the attention remains outside. In yoga, however, the attention is focused within oneself, depending on the specific yoga technique or meditation. This is why a person with high levels of stress and dissipation often finds yoga very difficult, although the practice in itself may not be difficult at all. By regular yoga practice and the combination of different systems of yoga, we gradually retrain the mind to become attentive and remain attentive at will. This attention, which is developed through yoga, is required in order to attain deeper experiences on the inner path. In fact, it is the quality of attention that determines the level of yoga that one has attained.

***Laziness***, the fourth obstruction, is the bane of all practitioners. The yogis of old aimed to practise for several hours daily. In order to achieve this, they had to adjust their diet and lifestyle, reducing outside activities to a minimum. The diet should be simple and bland; the lifestyle regulated and quiet. Meeting with family, friends and associates was deferred, so that more time could be devoted to solitude and practice. Although this may seem like the ideal sort of life for a yogi, it may also lead to laziness, because there is no external stimulation, no external demand or expectation to get one moving, to get things done. The yogi must find the motivation from within to follow the discipline and continue the practice, day in and day out. In the beginning the practice may go well, because one is strict about the regimen. But later on, there will be lapses. One will think, I don't want to practise just now. Maybe I can just sit in the sun and skip the practice. The mind can conjure up many excuses to take a rest or do something else. In this way, laziness slowly sets in. When this happens, the energy and the will power dissipate, and the practice becomes difficult to sustain.

***Sleep*** is the fifth obstruction. Here sleep does not just refer to the time one spends in bed at night, or even in naps during the day. The obstacle arises when one goes deep into meditation, and then sleeps intervenes. The purpose of yoga is ultimately to discover the more subtle states of consciousness, the subconscious, the unconscious and the superconscious. The problem arises, because these are the states normally reserved for sleep. When we enter these states, we habitually fall asleep. In the absence of an experienced teacher or guide, it is difficult to know whether the mind is awake and attentive or asleep in the deep states of consciousness. Even the yogi, who practises regularly and is able to enter the deeper consciousness at will, may succumb to sleep in these states, without knowing it. This can actually lead to regression in the path of yoga, and must be avoided.

But how to avoid it, when one readily falls into sleep. This is why intensive yoga practice was only recommended for advanced practitioners, who had control over wakefulness and sleep in all states and conditions.

***Irregular practice*** is the sixth obstacle in yoga. A regular practice, performed at regular times of the day, seems easy to follow. But again, over time, regularity in practice becomes very difficult to sustain. Regularity is one of the most important lifestyle observances. It is really the difference between success and failure in sadhana and higher yoga. In order to be regular in practice, one must be regular in all activities throughout the day: eating, sleeping, walking, talking, relaxing and exercising. Any lapse in regularity will disturb the practice. In fact, the smoother and more regulated the lifestyle, the deeper and easier the practice becomes. However, the mind is easily bored with this type of regulated lifestyle and practice, and seeks distractions and diversions in illusive ways. It gives many excuses to vary the routine, to have an outing, to meet with so and so. After some time, the constant barrage from the mind becomes overwhelming, and slowly one starts to give in. The practice will be done a little later, in the evening or tomorrow. First it happens once, then twice, and then, just like that, the practice is disturbed and upended.

***Confusion*** is the seventh obstacle. Confusion arises when we are unable to see things in their proper light. The classic example of this is a man, who is out walking late at night. Just ahead of him, he sights a large serpent in the middle of the road. He begins to tremble with fear and trepidation. As he approaches the location, however, he sees that the serpent is actually a long, thick rope, dropped by a passerby earlier in the day. In the same way, we are confused about many things in sadhana and in life. For example, we may mistake emotion for devotion; we may think that violent breathing is prāṇāyāma; we may mistake tamas in our practice for sattwa;

we may mistake egoistic feelings for exaltation. However, during a sustained yoga practice, even subtler confusions are sometimes experienced. We may see visions, hear voices, feel certain sensations or an unexplained presence, without knowing or understanding whether or not they are relevant or even real. We may enter into a state of total oblivion, and believe that we are in samādhi. This actually happened to our master, Swami Satyananda, when he was living with his guru, Swami Sivananda, in Rishikesh. Swami Sivananda immediately removed his confusion and instructed him about the correct way to practise in the future.

***Distress*** is the eighth obstacle. Although the practitioner may expect the outcome of sādhana to be enlightenment or ecstasy, it is often necessary to go through periods of distress, unease, anxiety and pain, due to the systemic changes that intensive practice may bring about. With the regular practice of sādhana, the psyche is stimulated and sensitised, causing many old, painful and traumatic memories to arise. These memories may be relived many times over with total clarity, as if the event or situation were happening at the present moment. One may think that sādhana would bring up the positive and pleasant memories, but it is often the exact opposite. Our subconscious is the storehouse of memories, and many of these are unpleasant. Some are traumatic and difficult to re-experience time and time again. These painful memories act as powerful toxins in the psyche and must be removed before higher experiences can be attained. This is one of the main causes of distress during the entire course of sādhana.

Another cause of distress is the process of spiritual awakening itself. Any sādhana, which is performed regularly, will bring about an awakening of the prāṇas, nāḍīs and cakras. In the beginning there will be major blockages in one or several of these subtle energetic areas. The elevated energy, awakened by the practice, must be able to pass through on its upward journey to the higher centres, located in the head region and at the crown. In the normal course of daily life, the energies are allowed to leak and dissipate, but the yogic practitioner must learn to conserve the energy and plug the leaks. This means that more energy becomes available, which must be properly directed. The correct channel for spiritual energy is suṣumnā nāḍī, the central passage in the spinal column. However, if there is any blockage or imbalance in the suṣumnā, the energy may then travel up the wrong pathway, perhaps iḍā or piñgalā, or another minor nāḍī in close proximity. Such an ascent of spiritual energy through the wrong channel can cause great distress on all levels, until the energy is brought back down and redirected up the proper channel.

Furthermore, there are nervous imbalances, which may arise due to irregular activation of the prāṇas and nāḍīs. These can cause distress at the mental and physical levels, which is difficult to treat by doctors or with medication. Introversion, depression, mood swings, restlessness, headaches, insomnia, diarrhea, constipation, infections, rashes, and pain of all kinds may arise without any external causes. During such times, one will have to ride it out, and keep faith in the power of the sādhana to restore the balance and regain the health. It may also become necessary to adjust or reduce the practice and the diet until the condition normalises.

***Lack of faith*** is the ninth obstacle. Faith is different to belief. Many practitioners may believe in the power and efficacy of sādhana, because they have heard or read about it from reliable sources. On the strength of this belief, they may wish to take up a regular sādhana. Faith, however, is based on one's own inner knowledge and experience. It is, therefore, unique to oneself and cannot be replicated or copied. Faith is the greatest wealth of the sadhak or yogi. Faith lends strength and steadiness to the practice, so that it cannot be given up on any account. In the absence of faith, the sadhak will lack determination, and the practice will become subject to outside influences, motivations and desires. Instead of practising, one may prefer to go out and meet someone or do something else. Faith binds the practitioner to the practice, and to the higher consciousness and divine powers from within, which sustain, guide and support the practice. In this way, the sādhana becomes a constant expression of love and pulls the practitioner along effortlessly into the higher domains of self realisation.

***Inability to attain the essence of yoga*** is the tenth obstacle, and also the culmination of all the above obstacles. Any one or combination of the above obstacles will lead the practitioner to this result. An inability to attain the subtle inner states and experiences of yoga is disturbing and disappointing for many practitioners. Some may even give up the practice on this account. One feels that inner progress is necessary and must be marked by certain experiences, just as outer progress is marked by certain gains in the external world. Because outer gains often take place in a relatively short period, one expects that inner goals should also be experienced in such time frames. However, the mind will only open when it is ready; in the same way that a flower blooms only in the right season. In order to realise the essence or truth of yoga, the limited individual mind must expand to encompass the entire universe and dimensions beyond. This is the unity of the individual consciousness with the supreme consciousness, of the individual self with the supreme self, or godhead. Only the sadhak with great patience and fortitude can think of ever attaining such essence or truth.

Thus, after reflecting on the above obstructions, the wise sadhak should forgo these ten obstacles.

## Verses 62 to 65: Merging apāna and prāṇa with agni

प्राणाभ्यासस्ततः कार्यो नित्यं सत्त्वस्थया धिया ।

सुषुम्ना लीयते चित्तं तथा वायुः प्रधावति ।।६२।।

शुष्के मले तु योगी च स्याद्गतिश्चलिता ततः ।

अधोगतिमपानं वै उर्ध्वगं कुरुते बलात् ।।६३।।

आकुञ्चनेन तं प्राहुर्मूलबन्धोऽयमुच्यते ।

अपानश्चोर्ध्वगो भूत्वा वह्निना सह गच्छति ।।६४।।

प्राणस्थानं ततो वह्निः प्राणापानौ च सत्वरम् ।

मिलित्वा कुण्डलीं याति प्रसुप्ता कुण्डलाकृतिः ।।६५।।

*prāṇābhyāsastataḥ kāryo nityaṃ sattvasthayā dhiyā*
*suṣumnā līyate cittaṃ tathā vāyuḥ pradhāvati* (62)
*śuṣke male tu yogī ca syādgatiścalitā tataḥ*
*adhogatimapānaṃ vai urdhvagaṃ kurute balāt* (63)
*ākuñcanena taṃ prāhurmūlabandho 'yamucyate*
*apānaścordhvago bhūtvā vahninā saha gacchati* (64)
*prāṇasthānaṃ tato vahniḥ prāṇāpānau ca satvaram*
*militvā kuṇḍalīṃ yāti prasuptā kuṇḍalākṛtiḥ* (65)

**Anvay**

*tataḥ*: thus; *prāṇa-abhyāsaḥ*: practice of prāṇāyāma; *nityam*: always; *kāryaḥ*: should be performed; *dhiyā*: by meditating on; *sthayā*: steadily; *sattva*: purity; *tathā*: then; *cittaṃ*: mind; *līyate*: is dissolved in; *suṣumnā*: suṣumnā; *vāyuḥ*: prāṇa; *pradhāvati*: pervades; *male śuṣke male*: when the impurities have withered away; *ca*: and; *gatiḥ-calitā*: with movement up; *tataḥ*: then; *syāt*: he becomes; *yogī*: yogin; *apāna*: apāna; *adhogatim*: moving downwards; *kurute urdhvagam*: should be raised upwards; *ākuñcanena prāhuḥ*: by contracting; *tam*: it; *balāt*: with force; *ayam ucyate*: this is called; *mūlabandhaḥ*: mūlabandha; *apānaḥ*: apāna; *bhūtvā urdhvagaḥ*: having been raised up; *gacchati*: moves to; *saha vahninā*: together with agni; *prāṇa-sthānam*: seat of prāṇa; *tataḥ vahniḥ*: then agni; *militvā*: having united; *prāṇa-apānau*: prāṇa and apāna; *satvaram*: quickly; *yāti*: goes to; *kuṇḍalīm*: kuṇḍalinī; *kuṇḍalākṛtiḥ*: coiled; *prasuptā*: fast asleep.

**Translation**

Thus the practice of prāṇāyāma should always be performed by meditating steadily on purity. Then the mind is dissolved in suṣumnā [and] prāṇa pervades [it]. When the impurities have withered away, and with movement up [the suṣumnā], he then becomes a yogin. Apāna moving downwards should be raised upwards by contracting it with force. This is called mūlabandha. Apāna, having been raised up, moves together with agni to the seat of prāṇa. Then agni, having united prāṇa and apāna, quickly goes to kuṇḍalinī [who is] coiled, fast asleep.

**Commentary**

In the 1900's when yoga was revived by international teachers coming out of India, and taught around the world, prāṇāyāma and meditation played a very minor role. Later on, many teachers began to teach yoga in their own countries, but their focus was āsana. They were not confident to teach prāṇāyāma, because their masters had not revealed it, and they did not understand the methods or scope of this practice. However, prāṇāyāma was gradually included in the yoga teaching as a mild form of breath control, for the purpose of physical benefits.

In early times, prāṇāyāma was considered to be *kumbhaka*, breath retention, and it played a considerable role in meditation and the awakening of kuṇḍalinī. This teaching relates to the period, when prāṇāyāma was used as a precursor to higher yogas. The instruction given on the awakening of the kuṇḍalinī begins with the practice of prāṇāyāma, which refers to kumbhaka, or breath retention.

When the breath is retained, or stopped, for an extended period, the mind also stops. Breath and mind function in tandem. When the mind stops, meditation occurs spontaneously, without the need for vigilance and control.

Thus, by the perfection of prāṇāyāma, the yogi was able to meditate steadily on the pure mind. In this way, prāṇāyāma was utilised as a form of meditation. The two practices, prāṇāyāma and meditation, were done in tandem for several hours at a stretch, until the mind dissolved into suṣumnā, the spiritual channel. Suṣumnā is pervaded by cosmic prāṇa. With the upward movement of this force, the mental impurities, which relate with the individual mind and consciousness, wither away. Henceforth, the mind of the practitioner is altered, and he becomes a yogi.

When this practice becomes steady, the course of apāna, the field of prāṇa, which normally flows downward in-between the waist and the pelvic floor, should be reversed and directed upward. This is achieved by redirecting the movement of energy together with the breath, and also by forceful contraction of the perineum, at the pelvic floor, which is known as mūlabandha.

When the energy of apāna is redirected upward, it unites with *agni*, the element of fire, behind the navel. Together the forces of apāna and agni merge with prāṇa at the maṇipura cakra. Having united with prāṇa and apāna, agni, quickly descends to the mūlādhāra cakra, where the kuṇḍalinī lies coiled, fast asleep.

***Technique***

Sit in a comfortable meditation āsana and relax the whole body from head to toe. Develop the awareness of steadiness and stillness. When the body is absolutely still, focus the attention on the breath. Practise slow rhythmic breathing through both nostrils until the breath becomes smooth and even.

Then apply the ratio with each breath, breathing in to the count of five and out to the count of five. When this ratio becomes effortless, add breath retention to the count of five after the completion of each inhalation. The ratio can be increased gradually, according to the capacity of the practitioner. After several rounds of practice, begin to pause in-between each round, for a few seconds. During the pause, breathe normally and become aware of the space of the mind. Then resume the prāṇāyāma practice. In this way, continue to practise prāṇāyāma together with meditation until the individual mind is dissolved into suṣumnā, and the thoughts have disappeared.

*Awareness of prāṇa vāyu:* Take the awareness to the field of prāṇa, in-between the diaphragm and the shoulders. Become aware of the upward flow of this field. Inhale slowly upward from the diaphragm to the shoulders, along with the flow of prāṇa. Imagine or feel waves of light, flowing together with the breath. Exhale back down. Feel the flow of light moving together with the breath from the shoulders to the diaphragm. Repeat the rotation of breath and light in this region until it becomes natural and spontaneous.

*Awareness of apāna vāyu:* Leave the region of prāṇa, and bring the attention to the area of apāna, in-between the waist and the pelvic floor. Here, see or imagine streams of light, flowing downward. Inhale downward slowly alongside the descending streams of light from the waist to the pelvic floor. Hold the breath inside and do mūlabandha, contraction of the perineum. Release mūlabandha and exhale back upward. Feel the flow of breath and light, moving upward together. At the end of exhalation, feel the force of apāna merging with agni, the element of fire, at the maṇipura cakra, behind the navel. Continue this rotation until it becomes spontaneous.

*Merging apāna and prāṇa with agni:*
While synchronising the movement of apāna with the breath,

simultaneously become aware of the movement of prāṇa. During inhalation, prāṇa moves upward and apāna moves downward. Visualise these two forces moving away from each other. At the time of exhalation, both flows are reversed. Prāṇa moves downward from the shoulders to the waist, and apāna moves upward from the pelvic floor to the waist. Imagine these two forces coming together at the navel. At the end of each inhalation, retain the breath and perform mūlabandha, contraction of the pelvic floor, for a few seconds. Release mūlabandha and exhale, merging the forces of apāna and prāṇa with agni at the navel.

*Descending of agni to kuṇḍalinī:* Be aware of the two distinct movements of apāna and prāṇa, moving away from each other on inhalation, followed by mūlabandha, and then the two forces come together and merge with agni at the navel. Each time apāna and prāṇa meet at the navel, feel the buildup of heat and light at the solar plexus, the center of prāṇa. Then agni having united with apāna and prāṇa quickly descends to mūlādhāra cakra, at the pelvic floor, where the kuṇḍalinī śakti lies coiled, fast asleep.

## Verses 66 to 69a: Awakening of kuṇḍalinī

तेनाग्निना च संतप्ता पवनेनैव चालिता ।

प्रसार्यं स्वशरीरं तु सुषुम्ना वदनान्तरें ।।६६।।

ब्रह्मग्रन्थिं ततो भित्त्वा रजोगुणसमुद्भवम् ।

सुषुम्ना वदने शीघ्रं विद्युल्लेखेव संस्फुरेत् ।।६७।।

विष्णुग्रन्थिं प्रयात्युच्चैः सत्वरं हृदि संस्थिता ।

ऊर्ध्वं गच्छति यच्चास्ते रुद्रग्रन्थिं तदुद्भवम् ।।६८।।

भ्रुवोर्मध्यं तु संभिद्य याति शीतांशुमण्डलम् ।६९।

*tenāgninā ca saṃtaptā pavanenaiva cālitā*
*prasāryaṃ svaśarīraṃ tu suṣumnā vadanāntareṃ* (66)
*brahmagranthiṃ tato bhittvā rajoguṇasamudbhavam*
*suṣumnā vadane śīghraṃ vidyullekheva saṃsphuret* (67)
*viṣṇugranthiṃ prayātyuccaiḥ satvaraṃ hṛdi saṃsthitā*
*ūrdhvaṃ gacchati yaccāste rudragranthiṃ tadudbhavam* (68)
*bhruvormadhyaṃ tu saṃbhidya yāti śītāṃśumaṇḍalam* (69a)

**Anvay**

*tena*: thus; *saṃtaptā*: heated; *agninā*: by agni; *ca*: and; *cālitā*: stirred up; *pavanena*: by vāyu; *tu*: now; *prasāryam*: stretches out; *sva-śarīram*: her body; *vadana-antarem*: inside the mouth; *suṣumnā*: suṣumnā; *tataḥ*: then; *bhittvā*: having pierced; *brahmagranthim*: psychic knot of creation; *rajoguṇa-samudbhavam*: produced by *rajoguṇa*; *saṃsphuret*: she blazes; *śīghram*: forthwith; *iva*: like; *vidyut-lekha*: stroke of lightning; *suṣumnā vadane*: at the mouth of suṣumnā; *satvaram*: immediately; *prayāti-uccaiḥ*: she proceeds up; *viṣṇugranthim*: through the psychic knot that sustains; *saṃsthitā*: abiding; *hṛdi*: in the heart; *gacchati*: she goes; *ūrdhvam*: upwards; *ca āste*: and continues; *rudragranthim*: through the psychic knot of duality; *yat*: which; *udbhavam*: comes from; *bhruvormadhyam*: eyebrow centre; *tu*: then; *saṃbhidya*: having pierced; *yāti*: she goes to; *śītāṃśu-maṇḍalam*: *maṇḍala* of the moon.

**Translation**

Thus [kuṇḍalinī], heated by agni and stirred up by vāyu, now stretches out her body inside the mouth [of] suṣumnā. Then, having pierced *brahmagranthi* produced by *rajoguṇa*, she blazes forthwith like a stroke of lightning at the mouth [of] suṣumnā. She immediately proceeds up through *viṣṇugranthi*, abiding in the heart. She goes upwards and continues through *rudragranthi,* which comes from the eyebrow centre. Then, having pierced [it], she goes to the *maṇḍala* of the moon.

**Commentary**

Many yoga practitioners ask about the process of kuṇḍalinī awakening; how does this cosmic force arise? Here the ascension of kuṇḍalinī is explained, following on from the previous verses. Agni, the element of fire, held by the maṇipura cakra, having merged with the combined forces of apāna and prāṇa vāyus, quickly descends to mūlādhāra cakra, at the perineum, where kuṇḍalinī śakti lies coiled, fast asleep. Kuṇḍalinī is heated by agni and stirred up by the vāyus, apāna and prāṇa. This causes her to awaken suddenly, and with an angry hiss, she enters the mouth of suṣumnā, located just above the mūlādhāra cakra. Inside suṣumnā she stretches out her coils and begins to ascend.

However, there are obstructions in her path in the form of the three *granthis*, or psychic knots, which bind her cosmic force in the world of creation. The first knot that she must pass through is *brahmagranthi*, the knot of creation. This knot is located in the region of mūlādhāra cakra, and relates with the reproductive drive, which is very powerful, especially in the early years. It is associated with *Brahma*, the lord of creation, and the desire for progeny that arises in all sentient beings. Under its influence, one feels the undeniable urge to reproduce oneself anew through the begetting of children. As long as this knot remains firm, the kuṇḍalinī cannot awaken fully and pass beyond the instinctive drives of mūlādhāra cakra, the root psychi c center. In order to loosen this knot, the serious yoga practitioner must be in control of the basic urges. Then only will the kuṇḍalinī will be able to pass through brahmagranthi, which is produced by *rajoguṇa*, the quality of dynamism and attraction to the world.

Having pierced through the brahmagranthi, the kuṇḍalinī then blazes forth from the mouth of suṣumnā, like a bolt of lightning. Thus, she immediately proceeds up the suṣumnā pathway to the second psychic knot, *viṣṇugranthi*, which is located in the region of anāhata cakra, behind the heart. Viṣṇugranthi represents the knot that sustains life, holding the individual in the world. Being located in the heart center, this knot relates with relationships and attachment to people, places and things. It encompasses all the love and affection one feels for family, home, work, friends, neighbours, pets, teachers, elders and so on. And conversely, all the disappointment, worry, anxiety, heart break, dejection and desolation, one may feel when there is loss or breakdown of any relationship. It is as if one's whole life is falling apart. In order to loosen this knot, the practitioner must develop one-pointed faith in and devotion to the divine self, or one's God in any form, which is most appealing. This follows the principle that lesser attraction succumbs to greater attraction.

Having pierced through viṣṇugranthi, the kuṇḍalinī continues on her ascent to the region of ajña cakra, behind the eyebrow center, where *rudragranthi* is located. Rudra is the lord of transformation or dissolution. This is the knot which binds one into the objective world of name and form. This world seems to be very real and permanent, as long as the rudragranthi holds one's perception firmly in the dimension of duality. When this knot becomes loosened, however, the unmanifest dimension unfolds. This is the reality behind the illusion of objectivity, which sustains the entire manifest creation. This knot may be terrifying for one, who is attached to the material world and all of its deceptive propensities. Therefore, it is called rudragranthi, the terrible knot, because by loosening it, one is catapulted into the void, beyond the senses and the mind, where there is nothing.

Then, having pierced rudragranthi, at the ajña cakra, kuṇḍalinī goes straight up bindu visarga, the point of light at the top back of the head, which is also known as the maṇḍala, or circle of the moon.

Symbolically, the moon represents the nectar of immortality. As long as the moon drips this nectar into the body, there will be prāṇa and life on the earthly plane. So, bindu is the source of life, through which the kuṇḍalinī first passes on its evolutionary journey, from cosmic existence to individual life. And again, she returns to bindu on her return journey at the time of enlightenment, or at the moment of death, when the soul passes out of the body.

## Verses 69b to 73: Falling of the nectar

अनाहताख्यं यच्चक्रं दलैः षोडशभिर्युतम् ।।६९।।
तत्र शीतांशुसंजातं द्रवं शोषयति स्वयम्
चलिते प्राणवेगेन रक्तं पित्तं रवेर्ग्रहात् ।।७०।।
यातेन्दुचक्रं यत्रास्ते शुद्धश्लेष्मद्रवात्मकम् ।
तत्र सिक्तं ग्रसत्युष्णं कथं शीतस्वभावकम् ।।७१।।
तथैव रभसा शुक्लं चन्द्ररूपं हि तप्यते ।
ऊर्ध्वं प्रवर्ति क्षुब्धा तदैवं भ्रमतेतराम् ।।७२।।
तस्यास्वादवशाच्चित्तं बहिष्ठं विषयेषु यत् ।
तदेव परं भुक्त्वा स्वस्थः स्वात्मरतो युवा ।।७३।।

*anāhatākhyaṃ yaccakraṃ dalaiḥ ṣoḍaśabhiryutam* (69b)
*tatra śītāṃśusaṃjātaṃ dravaṃ śoṣayati svayam*
*calite prāṇavegena raktaṃ pittaṃ ravergrahāt* (70)
*yātenducakraṃ yatrāste śuddhaśleṣmadravātmakam*
*tatra siktaṃ grasatyuṣṇaṃ kathaṃ śītasvabhāvakam* (71)
*tathaiva rabhasā śuklaṃ candrarūpaṃ hi tapyate*
*ūrdhvaṃ pravarti kṣubdhā tadaivaṃ bhramatetarām* (72)
*tasyāsvādavaśāccittaṃ bahiṣṭhaṃ viṣayeṣu yat*
*tadeva paraṃ bhuktvā svasthaḥ svātmarato yuvā* (73)

**Anvay**

*tatra*: there; *śoṣayati*: it dries up; *svayam*: by itself; *dravam*: fluid; *saṃjātam*: produced by; *śītāṃśu*: moon; *cakram*: in the cakra; *anāhata-ākhyam*: called *anāhata*; *yat*: which; *yutam*: has; *ṣoḍaśabhiḥ dalaiḥ*: sixteen petals; *raktam*: blood; *calite*: when agitated; *prāṇa-vegena*: through the force of prāṇa; *pittam*: bile; *grahāt*: through contact; *raveḥ*: sun; *yāta*: having gone to; *cakram*: sphere; *indu*: moon; *yatra*: where; *āste*: it exists as; *drava-ātmakam*: fluid nature; *śuddha-śleṣma*: pure phlegm; *katham*: how; *svabhāvakam*: by nature; *śīta*: cold; *grasati*: is converted into; *uṣṇam*: heat; *siktam*: it is poured out; *tatra*: there; *hi tathaiva*: in exactly the same manner; *śuklam*: white; *candra-rūpam*: form of the moon; *tapyate*: is heated; *rabhasā*: intensely; *tasya vaśā*: because of its desire for; *āsvadā*: enjoyment; *cittam*: mind; *yat bahiṣṭham*: is externalised; *viṣayeṣu*: among sensory objects; *yuvā*: aspirant; *bhuktvā*: enjoying; *tat param*: this high state; *svātmarataḥ svasthaḥ*: rejoices in [and] abides in the self.

**Translation**

There it dries up by itself the fluid produced by the moon in the cakra called *anāhata,* which has sixteen petals. The blood, when agitated through the force of prāṇa, [becomes] bile through contact [with] the sun, [then] having gone to the sphere [of] the moon, where it exists as the fluid nature of pure phlegm. How is [blood, which is] by nature cold, converted into heat [when] it is poured out there? In exactly the same manner, the white form of the moon is heated intensely. Because of its desire for enjoyment, the mind is externalised among sensory objects. The aspirant, enjoying this high state, rejoices in [and] abides in the self.

**Commentary**

During the normal course of life, the nectar from the the moon at bindu drips down into the body very slowly on a regular basis. First, it drips down into the field of consciousness in the head region, ruled by ajña cakra at the mid-brain, where it becomes the force for the individual consciousness and mind. This nectar of life has two propensities: *amṛta*, eternal life, and *viṣa*, poison or degeneration. As long as the nectar remains in the field of consciousness, the poison aspect is inactive. But the body must also be nourished and enlivened by this nectar. So, the nectar next drips down to viśuddhi cakra, behind the throat pit, which is the junction in-between the head and the body.

The word viśuddhi has two roots: *vi*, 'special' or 'complete', and *śuddhi*, 'purification'. When viśuddhi cakra is activated, it has the potential to collect the nectar and purify the poison, before it drips down into the body. However, if viśuddhi cakra is inactive, the poison passes straight through, along with the nectar. When this nectar mixed with poison falls down into the body, it becomes the source of life, as well as of degeneration and death. Having passed through viśuddhi cakra, the nectar next drips down to anāhata cakra, located behind the heart, where it is fanned by *vāyu*, the wind or air element. There, the fluid produced by the moon sustains the body, but it is also dried up by the wind, resulting in chronic and debilitating conditions, such as: nervous, cardiac, respiratory, and immune disorders, any of which may arise over time.

After passing through anāhata cakra, the remaining nectar then drips down to the region of the solar plexus, which is ruled by maṇipura cakra, where it becomes the storehouse of prāṇa in the body. Maṇipura holds the element of fire, or the sun, which is responsible for the process of metabolism and transformation. The nectar, which falls down into maṇipura, has two propensities, the red form and the white form. The red form becomes a catalyst for the production of blood, and is known as the red bindu. Agitated by the force of prāṇa, the blood, which is cold by nature, is transformed into bile and other gastric fluids through contact with the heat of the sun, or fire element.

The white form relates with the nectar from the sphere of the moon, which exists as the fluid nature of pure phlegm. The white form of the moon, or the white bindu, is also heated intensely due to desire for enjoyment. In this way the mind and senses are externalised amongst sensory objects, and move hither and thither in order to experience them. In the quest for further enjoyment, the white bindu falls down further to swādhiṣṭhāna and mūlādhāra cakras in the reproductive region, where it is transformed into semen andova. At this level the drive for sexual union becomes formidable, and the aspirant, enjoying this high state, rejoices in and abides in the self.

## Verses 74 to 76: Union of kuṇḍalinī with Śiva at mūlādhāra cakra

प्रकृत्यष्टकरूपं च स्थानं गच्छति कुण्डली ।

क्रोडीकृत्य शिवं याति क्रोडीकृत्य विलीयते ।।७४।।

इत्यधोर्ध्वरजः शुक्लं शिवे तदनु मारुतः ।

प्राणापानौ समा याति सदा जातौ तथैव च ।।७५।।

भूतेऽल्पे चाप्यनल्पे वा वाचके त्वतिवर्धते ।

धावयत्यखिला वाता अग्निमूषाहिरण्यवत् ।।७६।।

*prakṛtyaṣṭakarūpaṃ ca sthānaṃ gacchati kuṇḍalī*
*kroḍīkṛtya śivaṃ yāti kroḍīkṛtya vilīyate* (74)
*ityadhordhvarajaḥ śuklaṃ śive tadanu mārutaḥ*
*prāṇāpānau samau yāti sadā jātau tathaiva ca* (75)
*bhūte 'lpe cāpyanalpe vā vācake tvativardhate*
*dhāvayatyakhilā vātā agnimūṣāhiraṇyavat* (76)

**Anvay**

*kuṇḍalī*: kuṇḍalinī; *gacchati*: goes to; *sthānam*: place; *aṣṭaka-rūpam*: eight forms; *prakṛti*: nature; *ca*: and; *kroḍīkṛtya*: embracing; *yāti śivam*: attains Śiva; *vilīyate*: is dissolved; *iti*: thus; *śuklam rajaḥ*: white matter; *adhordhva*: falls down; *tadanu*: after that; *yāti*: goes; *mārutaḥ*: by means of the vital air; *śive*: to Śiva; *ca tathaiva*: and then; *prāṇa-apānau*: prāṇa and apāna; *sadā*: always; *jātau*: are produced; *samau*: equally; *ativardhate*: it transcends; *bhūte alpe*: whatever is small; *ca api analpe*: and even not small; *vā vācake*: or describable; *akhilāḥ vātāḥ*: entire prāṇa; *dhāvayati*: fires up; *hiraṇyavat*: like gold; *agnim-ūṣā*: earth's fire.

**Translation**

Kuṇḍalinī goes to the place [where she takes] the eight forms [of] nature, and, embracing [her Lord she], attains Śiva [and] is dissolved [in him]. Thus the white matter [which] falls down, after that goes by means of the vital air to Śiva, and then prāṇa and apāna are always produced equally. It transcends whatever is small and even not small or describable. The entire prāṇa fires up like gold [heated by] the earth's fire.

**Commentary**

In this way, the kuṇḍalinī descends on her journey of evolution in the form of *amṛta*, immortal nectar, creating and enlivening the form of the person, until she reaches mūlādhāra cakra, the center of *mūlaprakṛti*, the root essence of nature. There she abides in the eight forms of nature, the eight directions: east, west, north, south, north east, north west, south east, south west, and sustains the eight elements: earth, water, fire, air, ether, ego, memories and intellect. Although the kuṇḍalinī descends from the cosmic reality into the material dimension, she is never without her Lord. Even at the mūlādhāra cakra, Siva resides with her in the form of the smokey śivaliṅgam. Thus, taking the form of a tiny green serpent, the kuṇḍalinī settles into the earth and embraces her Lord. Coiling around him three and a half times, she dissolves into him and enters a dormant state of consciousness.

Therefore, the wise practitioner, who has understood this process, takes control over the sexual proclivities. The white bindu that falls down from manipura to mūlādhāra cakra should not be allowed to dissipate in sexual activities. Rather, it should be redirected upward by the prāṇa to the higher dimensions of Śiva. By redirecting the white bindu upward, the sexual and nervous energies become calm and balanced. This causes the pranic forces of prāṇa and apāna to be harmonised and equalised. When prāṇa and apāna are equalised, the mind becomes still and transcendent. The consciousness expands beyond the limitations of time, space and objects, whether small or large, describable or indescribable. The entire pranic system undergoes an awakening, and is fired up like gold, being heated by the kuṇḍalinī in the fire of the earth.

## Verses 77 and 78: Pranic body is the commander of all

आधिभौतिकदेहं तु आधिदैविकविग्रहे ।

देहोऽतिविमलं याति जातिवाहिकतामियात् ।।७७।।

जाड्यभावविनिर्मुक्तममलं चिन्मयात्मकम् ।

तस्यातिवाहिकं मुख्यं सर्वेषां तु मदात्मकम् ।।७८।।

*ādhibhautikadeham tu ādhidaivikavigrahe*
*deho 'tvimalaṃ yāti jātivāhikatāmiyāt* (77)
*jādyabhāvavinirmuktamamalaṃ cinmayātmakam*
*tasyātivāhikaṃ mukhyaṃ sarveṣāṃ tu madātmakam* (78)

**Anvay**

*tu*: then; *dehaḥ*: body; *ādhibhautika-deham*: body composed of elements; *yāti*: becomes; *ativimalam*: very pure; *ādhidaivika-vigrahe*: in a deified form; *ja-ativāhikatāmiyāt*: produced by its pranic body; *vinirmuktam*: released from; *jādya-bhāva*: dormant state; *cinmaya-ātmakam*: it consists of pure consciousness; *tasyāt*: thus; *ativāhikam*: pranic body; *mad-ātmakam*: being in the nature of the self; *mukhyam*: commander; *sarveṣām*: of all.

**Translation**

Then the body, [which is] a body composed of elements, becomes very pure in a deified form, produced by its pranic body. Released from the dormant state, it consists of pure consciousness. Thus, the pranic body, being in the nature of the self, [is] the commander of all.

**Commentary**

When the white bindu is redirected back up to its source, the prāṇas are harmonised. The material body comprised of the five elements (i.e.: earth, water, fire, air and ether) becomes absolutely pure, and assumes its divine form, produced by the subtle pranic body. With the purification of the elemental body, the entire pranic field undergoes an awakening, which is known as *prāṇottana,* awakening of the prāṇas. This pranic awakening precedes the awakening of kuṇḍalinī, and causes the kuṇḍalinī to uncoil her potential and enter the mouth of suṣumnā. As kuṇḍalinī ascends suṣumnā, the limited state of consciousness falls away, and the consciousness assumes its pure, expanded state.

Thus, it is said that the pranic body, being the nature of the self, or pure consciousness, is the commander of all. Prāṇa, being the nature of the self, is the first evolute of pure consciousness, and the source of all life and existence. Where prāṇa flows, there is life; there is existence. Where there is no prāṇa, there is no life. Nothing can exist in the absence of prāṇa. When the prāṇa flows downward into physical being, the consciousness becomes limited by the senses, and their perception of material existence. When the prāṇa is redirected upward, the consciousness is freed from the illusion of sensory perception, and the bondage of time, space and object no longer exist.

## Verses 79 to 81: Tearing asunder the veil of illusion

जायाभवविनिर्मुक्तः कालरूपस्य विभ्रमः ।

इति तं स्वस्वरूपा हि मति रज्जुभुजङ्गवत् ।।७९।।

मृषैवोदेति सकलं मृषैव प्रविलीयते ।

रौप्यबुद्धिः शुक्तिकायां स्त्रीपुंसोर्भ्रमतो यथा ।।८०।।

पिण्डब्रह्माण्डयोरैक्यं लिङ्गसूत्रात्मनोरपि ।

स्वापाव्याकृतयोरैक्यं स्वप्रकाशचिदात्मनोः ।।८१।।

*jāyābhavavinirmuktaḥ kālarūpasya vibhramaḥ*
*iti tam svasvarūpā hi mati rajjubhujangavat* (79)
*mṛṣaivodeti sakalam mṛṣaiva pravilīyate*
*raupyabuddhiḥ śuktikāyāṃ strīpuṃsorbhramato yathā* (80)
*piṇḍabrahmāṇḍayoraikyaṃ liṅgasūtrātmanorapi*
*svāpāvyākṛtayoraikyaṃ svaprakāśacidātmanoḥ* (81)

**Anvay**

*iti*: thus; *svasvarūpa*: one's true self; *tam*: this; *vinirmuktaḥ*: release from; *jāyā-bhava*: existence of a wife; *vibhramaḥ*: illusion; *kāla-rūpasya*: of the nature of time; *hi*: as; *mati*: belief; *rajju-bhujangavat*: rope like a snake; *sakalam*: all; *udeti*: arises; *eva mṛṣa*: indeed false; *pravilīyate*: dissolves; *yathā*: just as; *buddhiḥ*: idea; *raupya*: silver; *śuktikāyām*: in mother-of-pearl; *bhramataḥ*: illusion; *strīpuṃsoḥ*: of man and wife; *piṇḍa-brahmāṇḍayoḥ*: earth and cosmos; *aikyam*: one and the same; *api*: as; *liṅga-sūtrātmanoḥ*: soul which passes like a thread through the universe and its symbol; *svāpa-avyākṛtayoḥ*: sleep and the primordial spirit; *aikyam*: one and the same; *svaprakāśa-cidātmanoḥ*: light of consciousness and pure intelligence.

**Translation**

Thus one's true self [knows] this: the release from the existence of a wife, the illusion of the nature of time, as [is] the belief [that] a rope [is] like a snake. All [that] arises [is] indeed false; indeed [all that] dissolves [is] false. Just as the idea [of] silver in mother-of-pearl [is] an illusion, [so is that] of man and wife. The earth and the cosmos [are] one and the same, as [are] the soul which passes like a thread through the universe and its symbol. Sleep and the primordial spirit [are] one and the same, [as are] the light of consciousness and pure intelligence.

**Commentary**

Prāṇa is the first evolute of the self, or the consciousness. The entire manifest existence and all the beings within it depend on prāṇa. Hence, prāṇa is universal as well as individual. When the individual prāṇa is directed outside, one knows the external world, and its appearances seem to be very real. However, when the prāṇa is directed back to its source within, the true self is revealed. The higher consciousness then knows the appearance of form and object to be unreal and illusive.

In order to further elucidate this point, several examples are given, such as the release from the identity of wife or husband, father or son, friend or relative, etc. All the identities and roles that one assumes in life are actually transient and illusory. Being dependent on time, place and situation, they are impermanent and therefore unreal, just as the belief that a rope is a snake. All that is created and all that is dissolved is illusion, like the shimmer of silver in mother of pearl. Similarly, the idea of husband and wife is illusory and therefore, untrue.

The earth and the cosmos are one and the same, being of the same matter and origin. Similarly, the soul which passes through the universe, like a thread of consciousness, is the same as its symbol, the *liṅgam* (black oval). The state of sleep, being the deep unconscious, and the primordial spirit are also one and the same; as are the light of consciousness and pure intelligence. Light and intelligence both being the qualities of consciousness.

## Verses 82 and 83a: Śakti enters brahmarandhra

शक्तिः कुण्डलिनी नाम बिसतन्तुनिभा शुभा ।
मूलकन्दं फणाग्रेण दृष्ट्वा कमलकन्दवत् ।।८२।।
मुखेन पुच्छं संगृह्य ब्रह्मरन्ध्रसमन्विता ।८३।

*śaktiḥ kuṇḍalinī nāma bisatantunibhā śubhā*
*mūlakandaṃ phaṇāgreṇa dṛṣtvā kamalakandavat* (82)
*mukhena pucchaṃ saṃgṛhya brahmarandhrasamanvitā* (83a)

**Anvay**
*śaktiḥ*: śakti; *nāma kuṇḍalinī*: called kuṇḍalinī; *śubhā*: luminous; *bisatantu-nibhā*: like the lotus-fibre; *dṛṣtvā*: seeing; *phaṇa-agreṇa*: with the tip of her hood; *mūla-kandam*: bulb at the base; *kamala-kandavat*: similar to the bulb of the lotus; *saṃgṛhya*: grasping; *puccham*: tail; *mukhena*: with her mouth; *brahmarandhra-samanvitā*: she connects with the brahmarandhra.

**Translation**
The śakti called kuṇḍalinī, luminous [and] like the lotus-fibre, seeing with the tip of her hood the bulb at the base, similar to the bulb of the lotus, [and] grasping her tail with her mouth, she connects with the brahmarandhra.

**Commentary**
Kuṇḍalinī śakti is the cosmic creative force, which brings about all existence. Having created our physical being, she lies dormant within us at the *mūlakanda*, root or base, which is similar to the bulb of the lotus that remains rooted in the mud, beneath the water. The lotus, which grows up through the water and blooms on top, is sustained by the bulbous root beneath it. In the same way, our entire physical existence is created and sustained by the kuṇḍalinī śakti, who is luminous and bright, like the lotus fibre.

The dormant kuṇḍalinī is also described as a tiny green serpent, coiled three and a half times around the smoky black śivaliṅgam. There, at *mūlādhāra cakra*, the root center, she lies with her head on top of the liṅgam, asleep. However, her desire is not to remain in the earth forever. It is also her destiny to awaken within all beings, at some point in time. When her kinetic force begins to awaken, she sees with the tip of her hood the opening of the channel through which she descended, just above her head. Then, grasping her tail in her mouth, she enters the brahmarandhra, the subtlest channel inside suṣumnā, and prepares to ascend.

## Verses 83b to 87: Arising of kuṇḍalinī through the granthis and cakras

पद्मासनगतः स्वस्थो गुदमाकुञ्च्य साधकः ।।८३।।
वायुमूर्ध्वगतं कुर्वन्कुम्भकाविष्टमानसः ।
वाय्वाघातवशादग्निः स्वाधिष्ठानगतो ज्वलन् ।।८४।।
ज्वलनाघातपवना घातोरुन्निद्रितोऽहिरात् ।
ब्रह्मग्रन्थिं ततो भित्त्वा विष्णुग्रन्थिं भिनत्त्यतः ।।८५।।
रुद्रग्रन्थिं च भित्त्वैव कमलानि भिनत्ति षट् ।
सहस्राकमले शक्तिः शिवेन सह मोदते ।।८६।।
सैववस्था परा ज्ञेया सैव निर्वृतिकारिणी इति ।।८७।।

*padmāsanagataḥ svastho gudamākuñcya sādhakaḥ* (83b)
*vāyumūrdhvagataṃ kurvankumbhakāviṣṭamānasaḥ*
*vāyvāghātavaśādagniḥ svādhiṣṭhānagato jvalan* (84)
*jvalanāghātapavanāghātorunnidrito 'hirāt*
*brahmagranthiṃ tato bhittvā viṣṇugranthiṃ bhinattyataḥ* (85)
*rudragranthiṃ ca bhittvaiva kamalāni bhinatti ṣaṭ*
*sahasrākamale śaktiḥ śivena saha modate* (86)
*saivavasthā parā jñeyā saiva nirvṛtikāriṇī iti* (87)

**Anvay**

*sādhakaḥ*: yogin; *padmāsana-gataḥ svasthaḥ*: has taken his place in padmāsana; *gudam-ākuñcya*: anus contracted; *kurvan*: making; *vāyum*: vāyu; *ūrdhva-gatam*: go upwards; *mānasaḥ*: mind; *kumbhaka-āviṣṭa*: enter kumbhaka; *agniḥ*: agni; *vaśāt*: through the force; *vāyu-āghāta*: gust of vāyu; *svādhiṣṭhāna-gataḥ*: goes to svādhiṣṭhān; *jvalan*: in flames; *unnidritaḥ*: blowing; *jvalan-āghāta-pavan-āghātoḥ*: gusts of agni and vāyu; *ahirāt*: through the serpent; *tataḥ*: then; *bhittvā brahmagranthim*: having pierced brahmagranthim; *ataḥ*: next; *bhinatti viṣṇugranthim*: stabs viṣṇugranthi; *ca*: and; *bhittvā rudragranthim*: after piercing rudragranthi; *ṣaṭ kamalāni*: six lotuses; *Śaktiḥ*: Śakti; *Modate*: happy; *saha*

*Śivena*: with Śiva; *sahasrā-kamale*: in the thousand-petalled lotus; *iti*: thus; *jñeyā*: it should be understood; *sa parā avasthā*: this highest state; *eva*: alone; *kāriṇī*: produces; *nirvṛti*: bliss.

**Translation**

[When] the yogin has taken his place in padmāsana, his anus contracted, making the vāyu go upwards [and] the mind enter kumbhaka, [then] agni, through the force [of] the gust of vāyu, goes in flames to svādhiṣṭhāna. The blowing [of] the gusts of agni and vāyu through the serpent [which] then having pierced brahmagranthi, next stabs viṣṇugranthi and, after piercing rudragranthi, the six lotuses. [Now] Śakti [is] happy [to be] with Śiva in the thousand-petalled lotus. Thus it should be understood [that] this [is] the highest state; it alone produces bliss.

**Commentary**

The awakening and ascension of the kuṇḍalinī śakti from the earthly foundation to the divine is the goal of all yogas. Every yoga, every spiritual practice leads to this milestone in human evolution, however, kuṇḍalinī yoga is the most direct path. These verses, which complete the first chapter, describe the entire course of the awakening very succinctly and precisely.

***Technique***

The yogi, who has prepared and disciplined him/herself to undergo this process, should sit in padmāsana, or any comfortable meditative āsana, in a quiet and pure place, undisturbed by the trammels of life all around.

At first, one should be aware of the body, and relax it part by part from head to toe. Then become aware of the natural breath. Follow the movement of each breath with the awareness. Practice slow, rhythmic breathing until the mind and body become steady.

Bring the awareness down to the mūladhara cakra. Inhale slowly up through the perineum. Exhale back down again slowly. Continue to rotate the breath and the awareness up and down through the perineal body, and feel that you are piercing this region with each rotation.

Begin the practice of prāṇāyāma with kumbhaka. Inhale slowly through both nostrils and contract the anal sphincter. Redirect the *apāna vāyu* upward through the perineum with the ingoing breath. At the end of inhalation, retain the breath. Continue to hold the contraction and focus the attention on the state of kumbhaka. Experience the mind becoming absolutely still. Go deep into this stillness. Then exhale slowly through both nostrils, releasing the contraction. Direct the breath and the vayu back down through the perineum. Continue this rotation until the feeling of heat arises.

*Releasing brahmagranthi:* Next, visualise or imagine the *brahmagranthi,* psychic knot of creation, sitting like the bulb of a lotus, just above the mūlādhāra cakra. Continue the practice of pranayama with kumbhaka. While inhaling, feel the waves of apāna vāyu and *agni*, heat, arising together with the kuṇḍalinī śakti and piercing brahmagranthi. At the end of inhalation, hold the breath inside and experience the psychic knot opening. Exhale slowly back down through the brahmagranthi. Go on with this practice, until the knot is fully opened and there is no feeling of resistance.

Continue the practice of kumbhaka. While inhaling, experience the force of apāna vāyu, ascending in flames with the kuṇḍalinī serpent, through the sushumna pathway to svādhiṣṭhāna cakra, at the base of the spine. Retain the breath inside at svādhiṣṭhāna, and then exhale back down to mūlādhāra. Repeat this rotation until it becomes spontaneous. Then ascend in the same way to maṇipura chakra, behind the navel.

Having pierced brahmagranthi and the lower cakras with the

waves of vāyu and agni, the kuṇḍalinī serpent next arises to the region of anāhata cakra, behind the heart, and stabs *viṣṇugranthi*, the psychic knot of sustenance.

*Releasing viṣṇugranthi:* Now, focus the awareness at anāhata cakra. Visualise the viṣṇugranthi, sitting just above it, like the bulb of a lotus. Inhaling slowly upward through the anāhata cakra, direct a stream of golden prāṇa together with the luminous kuṇḍalinī śakti. Feel the psychic knot, situated just above, being pierced by the flow of prāṇa, kuṇḍalinī and breath. At the end of inhalation, retain the breath and experience absolute stillness. Then exhale back down through the psychic knot and the cakra. Go on with the practice, piercing viṣṇugranthi with each rotation until the psychic knot is released and holds no resistance.

Having pierced viṣṇugranthi, in the region of the heart, with the waves of golden prāṇa, the kuṇḍalinī next ascends to viśuddhi cakra, behind the throat.

Continue the practice of kumbhaka. While inhaling, experience the flow of prāṇa vāyu, ascending with the luminous kuṇḍalinī serpent through the suṣumnā pathway from anāhata cakra to viśuddhi cakra, unimpeded. At the end of inhalation, hold the breath and the awareness at viśuddhi. Experience vacuous space everywhere. Then exhale slowly back down through suṣumnā to the anāhata cakra. Repeat this rotation until it becomes spontaneous. Then ascend in the same way to ajña cakra, at the midbrain.

*Releasing rudragranthi:* Now focus the awareness at ajña cakra. Visualise the *rudragranthi*, psychic knot of dissolution, situated just above it. Inhaling slowly upward through ajña cakra, direct a stream of prana vāyu in the form of white light together with the luminous kuṇḍalinī śakti. Feel the psychic knot, situated just above, being pierced by the flow of white light, kuṇḍalinī and breath. At the end of inhalation, retain the breath and experience the light of consciousness. Then exhale back down through the psychic knot and the cakra. Go on with the practice, piercing rudragranthi with each rotation, until the psychic knot is released and holds no resistance.

After piercing the three granthis and the six cakras, Śakti easily makes her way unobstructed to sahasrāra cakra, the crown centre, where she is most pleased to unite with her Lord Śiva in the transcendent sphere of the thousand petalled lotus. This is the highest state, which alone produces bliss.

इति प्रथमोऽध्यायः ॥

*iti prathamo 'dhyāyaḥ*

Thus [ends] the first chapter.

द्वितीयोऽध्यायः

*dvitīyo 'dhyāyaḥ*

# Chapter Two

## Verses 1 to 4a: Khecarī vidyā

अथाहं संप्रवक्ष्यामि विद्यां खेचरीसंज्ञिकाम् ।
यथा विज्ञानवानस्या लोकेऽस्मिन्नजरोऽमरः ॥१॥
मृत्युव्याधिजराग्रस्तो दृष्ट्वा विद्यामिमां मुने ।
बुद्धिं दृढतरां कृत्वा खेचरीं तु समभ्यसेत् ॥२॥
जरामृत्युगदघ्नो यः खेचरीं वेत्ति भूतले ।
ग्रन्थतश्चर्थतश्चैव तदभ्यासप्रयोगतः ॥३॥
तं मुने सर्वभावेन गुरुं मत्या समाश्रयेत् ।४।

*athāhaṃ saṃpravakṣyāmi vidyāṃ khecarīsaṃjñikām*
*yathā vijñānavānasyā loke 'sminnajaro 'maraḥ* (1)
*mṛtyuvyādhijarāgrasto dṛṣṭvā vidyāmimāṃ mune*
*buddhiṃ dṛḍhatarāṃ kṛtvā khecarīṃ tu samabhyaset* (2)
*jarāmṛtyugadaghno yaḥ khecarīṃ vetti bhūtale*
*granthataścārthataścaiva tadabhyāsaprayogataḥ* (3)
*taṃ mune sarvabhāvena guruṃ matyā samāśrayet* (4a)

**Anvay**
*atha*: now; *aham saṃpravakṣyāmi*: I shall describe; *vidyām*: *vidyā*; *khecarī-saṃjñikām*: called *khecarī*; *yathā*: since; *asmin loke*: in this place; *amaraḥ*: no death; *najaraḥ*: no old age; *vijñānavānasyāḥ*: those who are endowed with this knowledge; *grastaḥ*: whoever is at the mercy of; *mṛtyu-vyādhi-jarā*: death, disease and old age; *dṛṣṭvā*: having learned; *imām vidyām*: this vidya; *mune*: o Sage; *kṛtvā dṛḍhatarām*: having strengthened; *buddhim*: mind; *tu*: then;

*samabhyaset khecarīm*: should practise khecarī; *matyā*: respectfully; *samāśrayet*: one should approach; *sarva-bhāvena*: with total devotion; *tam gurum*: the guru; *ghnaḥ*: destroyer; *jarā-mṛtyu-gada*: old age, death [and] disease; *bhūtale*: on earth; *yaḥ vetti khecarīm*: who knows khecarī; *arthataḥ*: meaning; *ca . . .ca*: both . . . and; *granthataḥ*: from books; *abhyāsa-prayogataḥ*: continual practice.

**Translation**

Now I shall describe the *vidyā* called *khecarī*, since [there is] in this place no death [or] old age [for] those who are endowed with this knowledge. Whoever is at the mercy of death, disease and old age, having learned this vidyā, o Sage, [and] having strengthened his mind, should then practise khecarī. One should respectfully approach with total devotion the guru, the destroyer [of] old age, death [and] disease on earth, who knows khecarī [and has learned] its meaning both from books and continual practice.

**Commentary**

*Khecarī mudrā*, the tongue lock, is one of the most highly venerated yoga practices. It is discussed at length in many of the upaniṣads, as well as in the classical haṭha yoga texts. There are two versions of this practice: the rāja yoga method and the haṭha yoga method. The rāja yoga method is used as an adjunct to prāṇāyāma, meditation and kriya yoga practices. It simply involves folding the tongue back, so that the under surface presses against the roof of the mouth, and the tip reaches into the region at the back of the throat. The haṭha yoga method involves gradual cutting of the frenum under the tongue, and is therefore irreversible. By systematic cutting, massaging and stretching, the tongue gradually becomes elongated and can reach into the nasal cavity. This position of the tongue activates ajña cakra and blocks the descent of the nectar and the consciousness into the lower centres.

The word khecarī comes from two roots: *khe*, meaning 'sky' and *carya*, meaning 'one who roams'. The yogi, who perfects khecarī, is considered to be liberated while living. He is able to roam freely in the space of consciousness, unaffected by the limitations and associations of the mind and the world. In the teachings given here, khecarī is described as a *vidyā,* knowledge that arises from within through practice and experience. Khecarī is said to be so powerful that old age and death cannot affect those who are endowed with this knowledge. Therefore, whoever is faced with disease, old age and death, should learn this vidyā, strengthen the mind, and practice khecarī. In order to learn khecarī, one should respectively approach the master, who has perfected it. Such a master, who knows the meaning of khecarī from books as well as from continual practice is regarded as the destroyer of disease, old age and death on earth.

### Verses 4b to 10: Importance of khecarī

दुर्लभा खेचरी विद्या तदभ्यासोऽपि दुर्लभः ॥४॥
अभ्यासं मेलनं चैव युगपन्नैव सिध्यति ।
अभ्यासमात्रनिरता न विन्दन्ते ह मेलनम् ॥५॥
अभ्यासं लभते ब्रह्मञ्जन्मान्तरे क्वचित् ।
मेलनं तत्तु जन्मनां शतान्तेऽपि न लभ्यते ॥६॥
अभ्यासं बहुजन्मान्ते कृत्वा तद्भावसाधितम् ।
मेलनं लभते कश्चिद्योगी जन्मान्तरे क्वचित् ॥७॥
यदा तु मेलनं योगी लभते गुरुवक्त्रतः ।
तदा तत्सिद्धिमाप्नोति यदुक्ता शास्त्रसंततौ ॥८॥
ग्रन्थतश्चार्थतश्चैव मेलनं लभते यदा ।
तदा शिवात्वमाप्नोति निर्मुक्तः सर्वसंसृतेः ॥९॥
शास्त्रं विनापि संबोद्धुं गुरवोऽपि न शक्नुयुः ।
तस्मात्सुदुर्लभतरं लभ्यं शास्त्रमिदं मुने ॥१०॥

*durlabhā khecarī vidyā tadabhyāso 'pi durlabhaḥ* (4b)
*abhyāsaṃ melanaṃ caiva yugapannaiva sidhyati*
*abhyāsamātraniratā na vindante ha melanam* (5)
*abhyāsaṃ labhate brahmanjanmāntare kvacit*
*melanaṃ tattu janmanāṃ śatānte 'pi na labhyate* (6)
*abhyāsaṃ bahujanmānte kṛtvā tadbhāvasādhitam*
*melanaṃ labhate kaścidyogī janmāntare kvacit* (7)
*yadā tu melanaṃ yogī labhate guruvaktrataḥ*
*tadā tatsiddhimāpnoti yaduktā śāstrasaṃtatau* (8)
*granthataścārthataścaiva melanaṃ labhate yadā*
*tadā śivātvamāpnoti nirmuktaḥ sarvasaṃsṛteḥ* (9)
*śāstraṃ vināpi saṃboddhuṃ guravo 'pi na śaknuyuḥ*
*tasmātsudurlabhataraṃ labhyaṃ śāstramidaṃ mune* (10)

**Anvay**

*vidyā khecarī*: vidyā [of] khecarī; *durlabhā*: difficult to attain;

*tat-abhyāsaḥ*: its practice; *api*: also; *durlabhaḥ*: difficult to attain; *abhyāsam ca melanam*: practice and melana; *na sidhyati*: are not accomplished; *yugapat*: at the same time; *niratāḥ*: those intent on; *abhyāsa-mātra*: practice alone; *na vindante melanam*: do not gain melana; *labhate*: one obtains; *abhyāsam*: practice; *brahman*: o Brahman; *kvacit*: at some time; *janmāntare*: in another life; *tu*: but; *na labhyate melanam*: one does not attain melana; *api*: even; *śatānte janmanām*: after a hundred lives; *kṛtvā*: having performed; *abhyāsam*: practice; *bahu-janmānte*: through many births; *tat-bhāvasādhitam*: perfected it; *kaścit yogī*: a yogin; *labhate melanam*: attains melana; *kvacit*: at some time; *janmāntare*: in a future birth; *yadā yogī labhate melanam*: if a yogin attains melana; *guru-vaktrataḥ*: from the mouth of the guru; *tadā āpnoti*: then he obtains; *tat-siddhim*: that *siddhi*; *yaduktā*: spoken of; *śāstra-saṃtatau*: in the eternal sacred teachings; *yadā labhate melanam*: if he attains melana; *ārthataḥ*: through its meaning; *granthataḥ*: in books; *tadā āpnoti*: then he reaches; *śivātvam*: Śiva; *nirmuktaḥ*: freed from; *sarva-saṃsṛteḥ*: all reincarnations; *api guravaḥ*: even gurus; *na śaknuyuḥ*: may not be able to; *saṃboddhum*: have this knowledge; *vinā śāstram*: without the sacred books; *tasmāt*: therefore; *mune*: o Sage; *idam śāstram*: this teaching; *sudurlabhataram*: very difficult to acquire.

**Translation**

The vidyā [of] khecarī [is] difficult to attain; its practice [is] also difficult to attain. Practice and *melana* are not accomplished at the same time. Those [who are] intent on practice alone do not gain melana. One obtains the practice, o Brahman, at some time in another life, but one does not attain melana even after a hundred lives. Having performed the practice through many births [and] perfected it, a yogin attains melana at some time in a future birth. If a yogin attains melana from the mouth of the guru, then he obtains that *siddhi* spoken of in the eternal sacred teachings. If he attains melana through its meaning in books, then he reaches Śiva [and is] freed from all reincarnations. Even gurus may not be able to have this knowledge without the sacred books. Therefore, o Sage, this teaching [is] very difficult to acquire.

**Commentary**
One may wonder why so much importance and respect were given by the yogis of old to this one practice of yoga. On closer examination, however, one can see that the experience of khecarī is indeed difficult to attain; even the practice is difficult to attain. Of course, the rāja yoga version can be done by anyone. Folding the tongue back, so that the tip reaches inward towards the throat cavity, has a calming and introverting effect on the mind. But the haṭha yoga method is not so easily achieved; it requires sacrifice and years of practice. The tongue must be gradually cut and stretched, until it can reach up into the nasal cavity, blocking the downward flow of the nectar and the connection of ajña cakra with the lower centres.

So, the practice of khecarī is one thing, and the *melana*, 'union' or 'coming together' that is achieved by establishing the position of the tongue at ajña cakra, is quite another. This union is also the definition of yoga, the union of the individual mind and consciousness with the supreme. Khecarī vidyā brings about this union by the activation of ajña cakra with the inverted and raised position of the tongue. However, the practice and the melana, or union, are not accomplished simultaneously. In fact, those who focus on perfecting the practice alone, do not attain the melana, or union. Khecarī is said to be so difficult that, although one may learn the practice in this life or in another life, the union or perfection is not acquired, even after one hundred lifetimes.

However, having performed the practice, and perfecting it over many births, the yogi will attain the union in a future birth. Another way to attain this melana, or union, is from the mouth of the guru, who has himself realised it. When the union is conveyed to the worthy disciple in this way, then he attains that spiritual power spoken of in the eternal sacred teachings. This melana, or union, may also be conveyed through its meaning in books. Then the yogi reaches *Śiva*, universal consciousness, and is freed from all further rebirths or incarnations. Even the gurus, self-realised masters, may not be able to acquire this knowledge without the sacred books. Therefore, this teaching is considered very difficult to attain.

## Verses 11 to 16a: How to acquire this knowledge

यावन्न लभ्यते शास्त्रं तावद्गां पर्यटेद्यतिः ।
यदा संलभ्यते शास्त्रं तदा सिद्धिः करे स्थिता ।।११।।
न शास्त्रेण विना सिद्धिर्दृष्टा चैव जगत्त्रये ।
तस्मान्मेलनदातारं शास्त्रदातारमच्युतम् ।।१२।।
तदभ्यासप्रदातारं शिवं मत्वा समाश्रयेत् ।
लब्ध्वा शास्त्रमिदं मह्यमन्येषां न प्रकाशयेत् ।।१३।।
तस्मात्सर्वप्रयत्नेन गोपनैयं विजञानता ।
यत्रास्ते च गुरुर्ब्रह्मन्दिव्ययोगप्रदायकः ।।१४।।
तत्र गत्वा च तेनोक्तविद्यां संगृह्य खेचरीम् ।
तेनोक्तः संयगभ्यासं कुर्यादावतन्द्रितः ।।१५।।
अनया विद्यया योगी खेचरीसिद्धिभाग्भवेत् ।१६।

*yāvanna labhyate śāstraṃ tāvadgāṃ paryatedyatiḥ*
*yadā saṃlabhyate śāstraṃ tadā siddhiḥ kare sthitā* (11)
*na śāstrena vinā siddhirdṛṣṭā caiva jagattraye*
*tasmānmelanadātāraṃ śāstradātāramacyutam* (12)
*tadabhyāsapradātāraṃ śivaṃ matvā samāśrayet*
*labdhvā śāstramidaṃ mahyamanyeṣāṃ na prakāśayet* (13)
*tasmātsarvaprayatnena gopanaiyaṃ vijñānatā*
*yatrāste ca gururbrahmandivyayogapradāyakaḥ* (14)
*tatra gatvā ca tenoktavidyāṃ saṃgṛhya khecharīṃ*
*tenoktaḥ saṃyagabhyāsaṃ kuryādāvatandritaḥ* (15)
*anayā vidyayā yogī khecarīsiddhibhāgbhavet* (16a)

**Anvay**

*yatiḥ*: ascetic; *gāṃ paryatet*: should go wandering; *yāvat tāvat*: for as long as; *na labhyate*: he does not have; *śāstram*: knowledge; *yadā*: when; *saṃlabhyate śāstram*: he does obtain the knowledge; *tadā*: then; *siddhiḥ sthitā*: siddhi is firmly; *kare*: in his hand; *tasmāt*: therefore; *acyutam*: Imperishable One; *śāstra-dātāram*: giving the teachings;

*melana-dātāram*: readily gives melana; *samāśrayet śivam*: he seeks refuge in Śiva; *matvā*: regarding; *abhyāsa-pradātāram*: bestower of the practice; *labdhvā idam śāstram*: having obtained this teaching; *mahyamani*: from the highly honoured ones; *na prakāśayet*: he should not reveal; *eṣām*: to others; *tasmāt*: therefore; *iyam vijñānatā*: this deep knowledge; *sarva-prayatnena*: with every effort; *gopana*: should be kept secret; *brahman*: o Brahman; *gatvā tatra*: having gone there; *yatra-āste*: where dwells; *guruḥ*: guru; *pradāyakaḥ*: imparts; *divya-yoga*: divine yoga; *ca*: and; *saṃgṛhya*: having comprehended; *khecharīm vidyām*: khecharī vidyā; *tena-ukta*: expressed by him; *ādau-atandritaḥ*: undaunted right from the start; *kuryāt*: one should do; *abhyāsam*: practice; *saṃyak*: correctly; *tena-uktaḥ*: as described by him; *anayā vidyayā*: through this knowledge; *yogī*: yogin; *khecarī-siddhi-bhāg-bhavet*: may become part of the siddhi of khecarī.

**Translation**

An ascetic should go wandering for as long as he does not have [this] knowledge. When he does obtain the knowledge, then the siddhi is firmly in his hand. Without this knowledge, the siddhi cannot be manifested in the three worlds. Therefore [it is] the imperishable one [who], giving the teachings, readily gives melana. [The yogin] seeks refuge in Śiva, regarding [him as] the bestower of the practice. Having obtained this teaching from the highly honoured ones, he should not reveal [it] to others. Therefore this deep knowledge should, with every effort, be kept secret. O Brahman, having gone there where dwells a guru [who] imparts the divine yoga, and having comprehended the khecarī vidyā expressed by him, one should, undaunted right from the start, do the practice correctly as described by him. Through this knowledge, the yogin may become part of the siddhi of khecarī.

**Commentary**

Khecarī vidyā in its full form is not intended for the worldly-minded practitioner, because cutting the tongue assures that communication with the world will also be cut. Therefore, the *yati*, or ascetic, who is disengaged from the activities of the world, should go wandering from place to place, until he acquires this knowledge. The imperishable one, being firmly established in the unchanging reality, who gives the teachings on this vidyā, also readily gives the melana.

When the yogi obtains this knowledge, spiritual power will be firmly in his hand. Without this knowledge, however, spiritual power cannot be manifested in the three worlds.

The yogi, who has received this knowledge, should take refuge in Śiva, regarding him as the bestower of the practice. Having received this deep knowledge from the highly honored ones, he should make every effort to keep it secret and avoid revealing it to others for any reason. Having reached the dwelling place of a guru, who imparts this divine yoga, one should listen carefully to the khecarī vidyā taught by him. Afterwards, one should find a suitable place and, undaunted right from the start, perform the practice correctly, as described by him. Through this knowledge, the yogi may become part of the powerful tradition of khecarī vidyā.

## Verses 16b to 18a: Khecarī bīja

खेचर्या खेचरीं युञ्जन्खेचरीबीजपूरया ।।१६।।

खेचराधिपतिर्भूत्वा खेचरेषु सदा वसेत् ।

खेचरावसथं वह्निमम्बुमण्डल भूषितम् ।।१७।।

आख्यातं खेचरीबीजं तेन योगः प्रसिध्यति ।

*khecaryā khecarīṃ yunjankhecarībījapūrayā* (16b)
*khecarādhipatirbhūtvā khecareṣu sadā vaset*
*khecarāvasathaṃ vahnimambumaṇḍala bhūṣitam* (17)
*ākhyātaṃ khecarībījaṃ tena yogaḥ prasidhyati* (18a)

**Anvay**

*pūrayā*: having expanded; *khecarī-bīja*: bīja of khecarī; *yunjan*: by uniting; *khecarīm*: khecarī; *khecaryā*: with the energy of khecarī; *bhūtvā*: he becomes; *khecarādhi-patiḥ*: Lord of the Khecaras; *vaset*: lives; *sadā*: forever; *khecareṣu*: amongst them (the Khecaras); *khecarī-bījam*: khecarī bīja; *ākhyātam*: is described as; *khecara-āvasatham*: abode of the Khecaras; *bhūṣitam*: adorned; *maṇḍala*: circle; *vahnim-ambu*: fire and water; *tena*: through this; *yogaḥ prasidhyati*: yoga is perfected.

**Translation**

Having expanded the bīja of khecarī by uniting khecarī with the energy of khecarī, he becomes Lord of the Khecaras and lives forever amongst them. Khecarī-bīja is described as the abode of the khecaras [and is] adorned [like] a circle [of] fire and water. Through this, yoga is perfected.

**Commentary**

The *bīja mantra*, or seed sound, of khecarī is *hrīṃ*. This bīja is expanded by uniting the practice of khecarī with the energy of khecarī, which is the kuṇḍalinī śakti. This means that with the perfection of khecarī, the practice itself becomes the final ascending energy of kuṇḍalinī, as she rises from viśuddhi cakra to pierce *lalana*, the nectar centre behind the throat, and then ascends to ajña cakra at the mid-brain. The yogi, who becomes established in the perfected state of khecarī, having thus awakened ajña, becomes lord of khecaras, and resides in the unconditioned state of consciousness all the time.

The khecarī bīja, *hrīṃ*, is described here as the abode of the khecaras. This means that the mantra is compounded from the sound *ha*, which represents the element of space, and khecara means one who roams, *cara*, in the *khe*, sky or space. The *ra* or '*repha*' sound is the state of fire, and the *ī* sound is adorned with the space of the moon (i.e. the *bindu* or *anusvāra* placed above the letter to indicate the *m* sound). In this way, the khecarī bija, *hrīṃ*, which grants perfection in yoga, is formed.

## Verses 18b to 21a: Esoteric details of the practice

सोमांशनवकं वर्णं प्रतिलोमेन चोद्धरेत् ॥१८॥

तस्मात्त्र्यंशकमाख्यातमक्षरं चन्द्ररूपकम् ।

तस्मादप्यष्टमं वर्णं विलोमेन परं मुने ॥१९॥

तथा तत्परमं विद्धि तदादिरपि पञ्चमी ।

इन्दोश्च बहुभिन्ने च कूटोऽयं परिकीर्तितः ॥२०॥

गुरूपदेशलभ्यं च सर्वयोगप्रसिद्धीदम् ।२१।

*somāṃśanavakaṃ varṇaṃ pratilomena coddharet* (18b)
*tasmāttryaṃśakamākhyātamakṣaraṃ candrarūpakam*
*tasmādapyaṣṭamaṃ varṇaṃ vilomena paraṃ mune* (19)
*tathā tatparamaṃ viddhi tadādirapi pañcamī*
*indośca bahubhinne ca kūṭo 'yaṃ parikīrtitaḥ* (20)
*gurūpadeśalabhyaṃ ca sarvayogaprasiddhīdam* (21a)

**Anvay**

*navakam*: ninth; *soma-aṃśa*: phase of the moon; *uddharet*: should be prounced; *pratilomena*: in reverse; *tasmāt*: then; *ākhyātam*: it is told; *akṣaram*: sound; *tri-aṃśakam*: three phases; *candra-rūpakam*: form of the moon; *tasmāt-api*: then also; *aṣṭamaṃ varṇam*: eighth sound; *vilomena*: in the opposite direction; *param*: supreme; *mune*: o Sage; *viddhi*: know; *tat-paramam*: it is supreme; *tat-ādih*: its beginning; *pañcamī*: fifth; *ca*: and; *ayam parikīrtitaḥ*: this is said; *kutaḥ*: peak; *indoḥ*: of the moon; *bahu-bhinne*: in its great part; *idam*: this; *prasiddhi*: success in; *sarva-yoga*: all yogas; *labhyam*: is to be gained; *guru-upadeśa*: through instruction by the guru.

**Translation**

The ninth sound [of] the phase of the moon should be pronounced in reverse. Then it is told [there is] a sound [made of] three phases [of] the form of the moon. Then also the eighth sound [pronounced] in the opposite direction [is] supreme, o Sage. Know [that] it is supreme [and] its beginning [is] the fifth, and this is said [to be] the peak of the moon in its great part. This [which gives] success in all yogas is to be gained through instruction by the guru.

**Commentary**

In order to reveal the precise meaning and method of practice referred to in the above verses, initiation of a guru in the khecara tradition must be sought. That teaching, which gives success in all yogas, is to be gained through direct instruction from the guru.

## Verses 21b to 24a: Benefits of the khecarī mantra

यत्तस्य देहजा माया निरुद्धकरणाश्रया ।।२१।।

स्वप्नेऽपि न लभेत्तस्य नित्यं द्वादशजप्यतः ।

य इमां पञ्च लक्षाणि जपेदपि सुयन्त्रितः ।।२२।।

तस्य श्रीखेचरीसिद्धिः स्वयमेव प्रवर्तते ।

नश्यन्ति सर्वविघ्नानि प्रसीदन्ति च देवताः ।।२३।।

वलीपलितनाशश्च भविष्यति न संशयः ।२४।

*yattasya dehajā māyā niruddhakaraṇāśrayā* (21b)
*svapne 'pi na labhettasya nityaṃ dvādaśajapyataḥ*
*ya imāṃ pañca lakṣāṇi japedapi suyantritaḥ* (22)
*tasya śrīkhecarīsiddhiḥ svayameva pravartate*
*naśyanti sarvavighnāni prasīdanti ca devatāḥ* (23)
*valīpalitanāśaśca bhaviṣyati na saṃśayaḥ* (24a)

**Anvay**

*tasya japyataḥ*: whoever repeats; *dvādaśa*: twelve; *nityam*: every day; *na labhet*: does not get; *api svapne*: even in sleep; *māyā dehajā*: *māya* born of the body; *āśrayā*: source; *niruddha-karaṇa*: hidden actions; *api suyantritaḥ*: and he who is self-disciplined; *japet*: repeats; *imām*: this; *pañca lakṣāṇi*: five hundred thousand times; *tasya*: to him; *śrīkhecarī-siddhiḥ*: siddhi of the glorious khecarī; *pravartate*: comes forth; *svayameva*: spontaneously; *sarva-vighnāni*: all obstructions; *naśyanti*: disappear; *ca*: and; *devatāḥ*: devas; *prasīdanti*: rejoice; *ca*: and; *na saṃśayaḥ*: without doubt; *bhaviṣyati*: there will be; *śaḥ*: elimination of; *valī-palitanā*: wrinkles and grey hair.

**Translation**

Whoever repeats [this] twelve [times] every day does not get even in sleep the *māya* [which is] born of the body [and] the source [of] hidden actions. And he who is self-disciplined repeats this five hundred thousand times, to him the siddhi of the glorious khecarī comes forth spontaneously. All obstructions disappear and the devas rejoice; and without doubt there will be elimination of wrinkles and grey hair.

**Commentary**

The yogi, who repeats the khecarī mantra, described in the previous verses twelve times daily, is freed from the bondage of maya, which is born of the body, and the source of all the hidden *samskara* and *karma*. The word *maya* means 'measured'. The spirit or soul of a person, being formless and timeless, is immeasurable and eternal. But when the spirit is born in a material body, it becomes bound by the physical form and its attributes, which are measurable and limited by time. Repetition of the khecarī mantras frees the practitioner from this bondage, even in the state of sleep and dream, which is very difficult to control, even for a yogi.

The disciplined yogi, who is able to repeat these mantras 500,000 times, will acquire the siddhi of khecarī spontaneously. All obstructions on the path of khecarī sādhana will be removed for him, and the divine beings rejoice in this attainment. These effects will also be experienced on the physical plane. There will be rejuvenation of the body and elimination of grey hair and wrinkles, without a doubt.

### Verses 24b to 27: Necessity of practice

एवं लब्ध्वा महाविद्यामभ्यासं कारयेत्ततः ।।२४।।

अन्यथा क्लिश्यते ब्रह्मन्न सिद्धिः खेचरीपथे ।

यदभ्यासविधौ विद्यां न लभेद्यः सुधामयीम् ।।२५।।

ततः संमेलकादौ च लब्ध्वा विद्यां सदा जपेत् ।

नान्यथा रहितो ब्रह्मन्न किंचित्सिद्धिभाग्भवेत् ।।२६।।

यदीदं लभ्यते शास्त्रं तदा विद्यां समाश्रयेत् ।

ततस्तदोदितां सिद्धिमाशु तां लभते मुनिः ।।२७।।

*evam labdhvā mahāvidyāmabhyāsaṃ kārayettataḥ* (24b)
*anyathā kliśyate brahmanna siddhiḥ khecarīpathe*
*yadabhyāsavidhau vidyāṃ na labhedyaḥ sudhāmayīm* (25)
*tataḥ sammelakādau ca labdhvā vidyāṃ sadā japet*
*nānyathā rahito brahmanna kiṃcitsiddhibhāgbhavet* (26)
*yadīdaṃ labhyate śāstraṃ tadā vidyāṃ samāśrayet*
*tatastadoditāṃ siddhimāśu tāṃ labhate muniḥ* (27)

**Anvay**

*labdhvā*: having obtained; *mahāvidyām*: great knowledge; *tataḥ*: then; *kārayet*: one should do; *abhyāsam*: practice; *anyathā*: otherwise; *brahman*: o Brahman; *kliśyate*: one will suffer; *na*: without; *siddhiḥ*: siddhi; *khecarī-pathe*: on the path of khecarī; *yaḥ na labhet*: whoever does not gain; *sudhāmayīm vidyām*: nectar-like knowledge; *yat-abhyāsa-vidhau*: through this cleansing practice; *labdhvā vidyām*: having gained it (the knowledge); *sammelaka-ādau*: at the beginning of melana; *japet*: should repeat; *sadā*: forever; *na-anyathā*: if not; *brahman*: o Brahman; *rahitaḥ*: who is lacking; *na bhavet*: does not get; *kiṃcit-siddhi-bhāg*: even a small part of siddhi; *yadi*: if; *labhyate*: he obtains; *idam śāstram*: this teaching; *tadā*: then; *samāśrayet*: he should practise; *vidyām*: knowledge; *tataḥ*: then; *muniḥ*: sage; *āśu*: quickly; *labhate*: obtains; *tām siddhim*: that siddhi; *uditām*: handed down.

**Translation**

Having obtained this great knowledge, one should then do the practice. Otherwise, o Brahman, one will suffer without [gaining] siddhi on the path of khecarī. Whoever does not gain this nectar-like knowledge through this cleansing practice, having gained it at the beginning of melana, should repeat it forever. If not, o Brahman, who is lacking it, does not get even a small part of siddhi. If he obtains this teaching, then he should practise its knowledge. Then the sage quickly obtains that siddhi handed down [to him].

**Commentary**

The khecarī mantras are the prelude to the practice of khecarī mudra. They set up the conducive vibrations within and all around the yogi, which allow this revered practice to be performed successfully. Therefore, the yogi who has acquired the knowledge of khecarī and repeated the specific mantras, should go on to perform the actual practice. Otherwise, one will continue to suffer on the wheel of birth and death, without ever gaining the ultimate liberation through the perfection of khecarī.

The knowledge of khecarī has been held in highest esteem from ancient times. Therefore, it remained secret, and was known to very few masters, who could pass it down in its entirety. For this reason, it is said that one who receives the direct experience of khecarī, even without the hidden knowledge of its background or mantras, should continue to practice it always. Otherwise, in the absence of khecarī, the yogi will not attain even a fraction of perfection. The yogi, who is fortunate to receive this teaching, should practise it. Then he will quickly obtain the perfection of yoga, which has been handed down to him.

## Verses 28 to 37a: Method of khecarī

तालुमूलं समुत्कृष्य सप्तवासरमात्मवित् ।
स्वगुरूक्तप्रकारेण मलं सर्वं विशोधयेत् ।।२८।।
स्नुहिपत्रनिभं शस्त्रं सुतीक्ष्णं स्निग्धनिर्मलम् ।
समादाय ततस्तेन रोममात्रं समुच्छिनेत् ।।२९।।
हित्वा सैन्धवपथ्याभ्यां चूर्णिताभ्यां प्रकर्षयेत् ।
पुनः सप्तदिने प्राप्ते रोममात्रं समुच्छिनेत् ।।३०।।
एवं क्रमेण षन्मासं नित्योद्‌युक्तः समाचरेत् ।
षण्मासाद्रसनामूलं शिराबद्‌धं प्रणश्यति ।।३१।।
अथ वागीश्वरीधाम शिरो वस्त्रेण वेष्टयेत् ।
शनैरुत्कर्षयेद्‌योगी कालवेलाविधानवित् ।।३२।।
पुनः षण्मासमात्रेण नित्यं संघर्षणान्मुने ।
भ्रूमध्यावधि चाप्येति तिर्यक्कर्णबिलावधिः ।।३३।।
अधश्च चुबुकं मूलं प्रयाति क्रमचारिता ।
पुनः संवत्सराणां तु तृतीयादेव लीलया ।।३४।।
केशान्तमूर्ध्वं क्रामति तिर्यक्शाखावधिर्मुने ।
अधस्तात्कण्ठकूपान्तं पुनर्वर्षत्रयेण तु ।।३५।।
ब्रह्मरन्ध्रं समावृत्य तिष्ठेदेव न संशयः ।
तिर्यक् चूलितलं याति अधः कण्ठबिलावधि ।।३६।।
शनैः शनैर्मस्तकाच्च महावज्रकपाटभित् ।३७।

*tālumūlaṃ samutkṛṣya saptavāsaramātmavit*
*svagurūktaprakāreṇa malaṃ sarvaṃ viśodhayet* (28)
*snuhipatranibhaṃ śastraṃ sutīkṣṇaṃ snigdhanirmalam*
*samādāya tatastena romamātraṃ samucchinet* (29)
*hitvā saindhavapathyābhyāṃ cūrnitābhyāṃ prakarṣayet*
*punaḥ saptadine prāpte romamātraṃ samucchinet* (30)
*evaṃ krameṇa ṣanmāsaṃ nityodyuktaḥ samācaret*

*ṣanmāsādrasanāmūlaṃ śirābaddhaṃ pranaśyati* (31)
*atha vāgīśvarīdhāma śiro vastreṇa veṣṭayet*
*śanairutkarṣayedyogī kālavelāvidhānavit* (32)
*punaḥ ṣanmāsamātreṇa nityaṃ saṃgharṣaṇānmune*
*bhrūmadhyāvadhi cāpyeti tiryakkarṇabilāvadhiḥ* (33)
*adhaśca cubukaṃ mūlaṃ prayāti kramacāritā*
*punaḥ saṃvatsarāṇāṃ tu tṛtīyādeva līlayā* (34)
*keśāntamūrdhvaṃ krāmati tiryakśākhāvadhirmune*
*adhastātkaṇṭhakūpāntaṃ punarvarṣatrayeṇa tu* (35)
*brahmarandhraṃ samāvṛtya tiṣṭhedeva na saṃśayaḥ*
*tiryak cūlitalaṃ yāti adhaḥ kaṇṭhabilāvadhi* (36)
*śanaiḥ śanairmastakācca mahāvajrakapātabhit* (37a)

**Anvay**

*samutkṛṣya*: having drawn up; *tālu-mūlam*: root of the palate; *ātmavit*: knower of atman; *sapta-vāsaram*: for seven days; *viśodhayet*: should clear; *sarvam malam*: every impurity; *prakāreṇa*: in the way; *svaguru-ukta*: described by his guru; *nirmalam*: clean; *snigdha*: oiled; *sutīkṣṇam*: sharp; *śastram*: knife; *nibham*: resembling; *snuhi-patra*: leaf of the *snuhi* plant; *tataḥ*: then; *samādāya tena*: with it; *samucchinet*: he should cut off; *roma-mātram*: size of a hair; *prāpte sapta-dine*: when he has completed the seventh day; *punaḥ*: again; *samucchinet*: he should cut off; *roma-mātram*: size of a hair; *evam*: so; *nitya-udyuktaḥ*: having made constant effort; *samācaret*: he should continue; *krameṇa*: steadily; *ṣan-māsāt*: in six months; *rasanā-mūlam*: root of the organ of taste; *śirā-baddham*: attached to the head; *pranaśyati*: is destroyed; *atha yogī*: then the yogin; *kāla-velā-vidhāna-vit*: who knows the right time and method; *veṣṭayet*: should enclose; *vastreṇa*: with cloth; *śiraḥ*: head; *dhāma*: mighty; *vāk-īśvarī*: Lord of Speech; *śanaiḥ*: slowly; *utkarṣayet*: elevating; *punaḥ*: again; *nityam saṃgharṣaṇāt*: through daily friction; *ṣan-māsa-mātreṇa*: for a period of six months; *mune*: o Sage; *āpyeti*: it reaches; *bhrūmadhya-avadhi*: up to the eyebrow centre; *ca*: and; *tiryak*: sideways; *karṇa-bila-avadhiḥ*: up to the opening of the ears; *ca adhaḥ*: and then; *krama-cāritā*: gradually set in motion; *prayāti*: it proceeds to; *mūlam*: root; *cubukam*: chin; *tu punaḥ*: then again; *tṛtīyāt saṃvatsarāṇām*: after the third year; *krāmati*: it progresses to; *līlayā*: easily; *ūrdhvam*: upwards; *keśāntam*: where the hair meets the forehead; *tiryak*: sideways; *śākhā-avadhiḥ*: up to the aperture at the top back of the head; *mune*: o Sage; *adhastāt*: downwards to; *kaṇṭha-kūpāntam*: throat-pit; *punaḥ-varṣa-trayeṇa*: in another three years; *brahmarandhram samāvṛtya*: having reached *brahmarandhra*; *na saṃśayaḥ*: without doubt; *tiṣṭhet-eva*: it remains there; *yāti*: it goes to; *tiryak*: sideways; *cūli-talam*: beneath the crest of hair; *adhaḥ*: downwards; *kaṇṭha-kūpāntam-avadhi*: right to the throat-pit; *ca śanaiḥ śanaiḥ*: and very slowly; *mahā-vajra-kapātabhit*: through the great adamantine doors; *mastakāt*: of the skull.

**Translation**

Having drawn up [the tongue from] the root of the palate, the knower of ātman should for seven days clear every impurity [from it] in the way described by his guru. [He should take] a clean, oiled and sharp knife resembling the leaf of the *snuhi* plant, then with it [make a] cut the size of a hair. He should quickly apply [it] with crushed rock-salt and sea-salt. When he has completed the seventh day, he should again cut off [a piece] the size of a hair. So, having made constant effort, he should continue steadily. In six months the root of the organ of taste attached to the head is destroyed. Then the yogin who knows the right time and method should enclose with cloth the head [of] the mighty Lord of Speech, slowly elevating [it]. Again through daily friction for a period of six months, o Sage, it reaches up to the eyebrow centre and sideways up to the opening of the ears. And then, gradually set in motion, it proceeds to the root [of] the chin. Then again, after the third year, it progresses easily upwards to where the hair meets the forehead, [then] sideways up to s*hakha,* the aperture at the top back of the head, o Sage, [and] downwards to the throat-pit. In another three years, having reached *brahmarandhra*, it without doubt remains there. It goes sideways to beneath the crest of hair, downwards right to the throat-pit and very slowly through the great adamantine doors of the skull.

**Technique**

*Stage one, purifying the tongue:* The tongue should first be cleaned with a tooth brush or a metal tool, called a tongue scraper. This should be done daily in the early morning to clear away all impurities. Next the tongue may be oiled, massaged and pulled in order to loosen it from the root or base of the mouth. This initial purification should be performed daily for at least 7 days.

*Stage two, preliminary practice:* Sit in a comfortable meditative asana with the back straight. Head neck and shoulders should be in alignment with the back. The hands should be placed on the knees in chin or jnana mudra. Relax the whole body and close the eyes. Fold the tongue upward and backward, so that the lower surface lies in contact with the roof of the mouth. Stretch the tip of the tongue back towards the opening of the throat. Hold the position with the tongue as far back as comfortable. Breathe slowly and deeply. When the tongue becomes tired, release and relax it. Then repeat the practice.

*Stage three, cutting the frenum:* Using a clean, oiled and sharp knife or razor, make a tiny incision into the frenum, no larger than the width of a hair. Quickly apply crushed rock salt or sea salt to the cut. After seven days, when the cut has healed over, make another hair width incision. Continue in the same way steadily for six months, until the root of the tongue that attaches it to the base of the mouth, is severed.

*Stage four, elongating the tongue externally:* Fold a small cloth around the tongue and slowly begin to manipulate it. Pull gently on the tongue and stretch it outward and upward. Continue this practice daily. After a period of six months, the tip of the tongue will reach upward to the eyebrow center, sideways to the opening of the ears, and downward to the base of the chin. After three years, with regular practice, the tongue will easily reach upward to where the hairline meets the forehead, sideways to the top back of the head, where the brahmins keep a tuft, and downward to the throat-pit.

*Stage five, rotating the tongue internally:* Manually insert the tongue into the aperture at the back of the throat and begin to feed it upward internally. After another three years, the tip of the tongue will reach the *brahmarandhra*, at the crown of the head, where the fontanelle is located. It will remain there, without a doubt, for as long as one chooses. The tongue will also move sideways to the point beneath the crest of hair, and very slowly right down through the doors of the skull to the throat-pit.

## Verses 37b to 40a: Practise slowly

पूर्वं बीजयुता विद्या ह्याख्याता यातिदुर्लभा ।।३७।।
तस्याः षडङ्गं कुर्वातं तया षट्स्वरभिन्नया ।
कुर्यादेवं करन्यासं सर्वसिद्ध्यादिहेतवे ।।३८।।
शनैरेवं प्रकर्तव्यमभ्यासं युगपन्नहि ।
युगपद्वर्तते यस्य शरीरं विलयं व्रजेत् ।।३९।।
तस्माच्छनैः शनैः कार्यमभ्यासं मुनिपुङ्गव ।४०।

*pūrvam bījayutā vidyā hyākhyātā yātidurlabhā* (37b)
*tasyāḥ ṣadaṅgaṃ kurvātaṃ tayā ṣaṭsvarabhinnayā*
*kuryādevaṃ karanyāsaṃ sarvasiddhyādihetave* (38)
*śanairevaṃ prakartavyamabhyāsaṃ yugapannahi*
*yugapadvartate yasya śarīraṃ vilayaṃ vrajet* (39)
*tasmācchanaiḥ śanaiḥ kāryamabhyāsaṃ munipuṅgava* (40a)

**Anvay**

*vidyā bīja-yutā*: knowledge concerning the seed sound; *ākhyātā*: was explained; *pūrvam*: previously; *yāti hi durlabhā*: is indeed extraordinary; *kurvātam*: one should do; *ṣat-aṅgam*: six parts; *tasyāḥ*: of this; *tayā ṣaṭ-svara-bhinnayā*: through its six different tones; *kuryāt*: one should do; *karanyāsam*: mystic hand movements; *hetave*: for the purpose of; *sarva-siddhi-ādi*: all the first siddhis; *evam abhyāsam*: this practice; *prakartavyam*: should be prepared; *śanaiḥ*: slowly; *na yugapat*: not all at the same time; *hi*: since; *śarīram*: body; *yasya*: which; *vartate*: practises; *yugapat*: all at once; *vilayam vrajet*: quickly decomposes; *tasmāt*: therefore; *abhyāsam*: practice; *kāryam*: should be done; *śanaiḥ śanaiḥ*: very gradually; *munipuṅgava*: o Esteemed Sage.

**Translation**

The knowledge concerning the seed sound, [which] was explained previously, is indeed extraordinary. One should do the six parts of this [vidyā] through its six different tones.
One should do mystic hand movements for the purpose of

[attaining] all the first siddhis. This practice should be prepared slowly [and] not all at the same time, since the body which practises [it] all at once quickly decomposes. Therefore, the practice should be done very gradually, o Esteemed Sage.

**Commentary**

Khecarī is the main yoga practice found in the yoga upaniṣads. Today, only the first two stages described in the previous section are generally practised and taught. However, when undertaken in its full form each stage of khecarī needs to be done slowly and methodically, under the guidance of an experienced master. The meaning of the word *khecarī* is very relevant here. One who perfects this practice is able to roam freely in the vast sky of consciousness, unfettered by worldly associations and limitations. In this sense, khecarī is synonymous with *mokṣa,* because it bestows liberation on its practitioners.

Liberation means to soar free from the bondage, the karma, the gravitational pull of the material world. However, the full practice of khecarī is not intended for those who are actively engaged in the world, because the faculties of speech and swallowing are seriously obstructed. Khecarī redirects the energy of viśuddhi cakra back upward to the field of consciousness, before it falls down into the lower centres and becomes identified or associated with the external world. As long as the full form of khecarī is maintained, one is able to roam freely in the vast sky of consciousness without any mental disturbance or dissipation.

## Verses 40b to 44a: Last stage of khecarī

तदा च बाह्यमार्गेण जिह्वा ब्रह्मबिलं व्रजेत् ।।४०।।

तदा ब्रह्मार्गलं ब्रह्मन्दुर्भेद्यं त्रिदशनैरपि ।

अङ्गुल्यग्रेण संघृष्य जिह्वामात्रं निवेशयेत् ।।४१।।

एवं वर्षत्रयं कृत्वा ब्रह्मद्वारं प्रविश्यति ।

ब्रह्मद्वारे प्रविष्टे तु सम्यङ्मथनमाचरेत् ।।४२।।

मथनेन विना किञ्चित्साधयन्ति विपश्चिताः ।

खेचरीमन्त्रसिद्धस्य सिध्यां मथनेन विना ।।४३।।

जपं च मथनं चैव कृत्वा शीघ्रं फलं लभेत् ।४४।

*tadā ca bāhyamārgeṇa jihvā brahmabilaṃ vrajet* (40b)
*tadā brahmārgalaṃ brahmandurbhedyaṃ tridaśanairapi*
*aṅgulyagreṇa saṃghṛṣya jihvāmātraṃ niveśayet* (41)
*evaṃ varṣatrayaṃ kṛtvā brahmadvāraṃ praviśyati*
*brahmadvāre praviṣṭe tu samyaṅmathanamācaret* (42)
*mathanena vinā kiñcitsādhayanti vipaścitāḥ*
*khecarīmantrasiddhasya sidhyāṃ mathanena vinā* (43)
*japaṃ ca mathanaṃ caiva kṛtvā śīghraṃ phalaṃ labhet* (44a)

**Anvay**

*tadā*: then; *jihvā*: tongue; *vrajet*: moves to; *brahmabilam*: brahmarandhra; *bāhya-mārgeṇa*: through the outer path; *ca tadā*: and then; *saṃghṛṣya*: having been rubbed; *aṅgulyagreṇa*: with the finger-tip; *brahmārgalam*: bolt of Brahma; *durbhedyam*: is difficult to be pierced; *api*: even; *brahman tridaśanaiḥ*: by the gods; *niveśayet*: enters; *jihvā-mātram*: space of the tongue; *kṛtvā evam*: having done this; *varṣa-trayam*: for three years; *praviśyati*: it moves through; *brahma-dvāram*: entrance to Brahma; *tu*: now; *praviṣṭe*: having moved through; *brahma-dvāre*: entrance to Brahma; *mathanam-acaret*: it performs rubbing, churning; *samyak*: perfectly; *vipaścitāḥ*: inspired people; *kiñcit*: sometimes; *sādhayanti*: reach the goal; *mathanena vinā*: without rubbing or churning; *khecarī-mantra-siddhasya*: whoever masters khecarī mantra; *sidhyām*: may attain; *mathanena vinā*: without churning; *labhet*: one obtains; *phalam*: fruits; *śīghram*: quickly; *kṛtvā*: by doing; *japam ca mathanam ca*: both repetition of mantra and churning.

**Translation**

Then the tongue moves to the brahmarandhra through the outer path. And then, having been rubbed with the finger-tips, the tongue enters the bolt of Brahma, [which] is difficult to be pierced even by the gods. Having done this for three years, it moves through to the entrance to Brahma. Now, having moved through to the entrance to Brahma, it performs churning perfectly. Inspired people sometimes reach the goal without churning. Whoever masters khecarī mantra may attain without churning. One obtains the fruits quickly by doing both repetition of mantra and churning.

**Commentary**

These verses describe stage five of the practice given in the previous section. This stage can only be applied after the frenum has been gradually cut and the tongue elongated in the systematic manner detailed above. Then the tongue is massaged with the fingertips and pushed methodically inward and upward through the outer path, ie. the opening at the back of the throat. When the elongated tongue reaches ajña cakra, at the mid-brain, the yogi experiences the 'bolt of brahma', allowing him to transcend the mind and enter the space of consciousness. This space is highly revered and is said to be difficult to attain, even by the gods.

After performing this practice on a regular basis for three years, the tongue moves further upward to the *brahmarandhra*, at the top back of the head, where the fontanelle is located. This point is also known as bindu cakra, from which the spirit descends into the body before birth and leaves the body at the time of death. In the above verses this point is called the ‘entrance to Brahma’, because it represents the source of individual consciousness and creation. Beyond this point there is nothing: no name, no form, no ideation, only brahman, ever expanding cosmic consciousness, pure and absolute.

Now, having reached the brahmarandhra, at the top back of the head, the tongue performs perfect and spontaneous churning in order to gain access to the cosmic consciousness beyond. Some yogis may reach this pinnacle, even without churning. It is said that whoever masters the khecarī mantra may attain this state without churning. However, one obtains the goal more quickly by utilising both the repetition of the mantra and the churning.

## Verses 44b to 49: Sūtra neti, adjunct to khecarī

स्वर्णजां रौप्यजां वापि लोहजां वा शलाकिकाम् ।।४४।।
नियोच्य नासिकारन्ध्रं दुग्ध सिक्तेन तन्तुना ।
प्राणान्निरुध्य हृदये सुखमासनमात्मनः ।।४५।।
शनैः सुमथनं कुर्याद्भ्रूमध्ये न्यस्य चक्षुषी ।
षण्मासं मथनावस्था भावेनैव प्रजायते ।।४६।।
यथा सुषुप्तिर्बालानां यथा भवस्तथा भरेत् ।
न सदा मथनं शस्तं मासे समाचरेत् ।।४७।।
सदा रसनया योगी मार्गं न परिसंक्रमेत् ।
एवं द्वादशवर्षान्ते संसिद्धिर्भवति ध्रुवा ।।४८।।
शरिरे सकलं विश्वं पश्यन्त्यात्माविभेदतः ।
ब्रह्माण्डोऽयं महामार्गो राजदन्तोर्ध्वकुण्डली ।।४९।। इति ।।

*svarnajāṃ raupyajāṃ vāpi lohajāṃ vā śalākikām* (44b)
*niyojya nāsikārandhraṃ dugdha siktena tantunā*
*prāṇānnirudhya hṛdaye sukhamāsanamātmanaḥ* (45)
*śanaiḥ sumathanaṃ kuryādbhrūmadhye nyasya cakṣuṣī*
*ṣaṇmāsaṃ mathanāvasthā bhāvenaiva prajāyate* (46)
*yathā suṣuptirbālānāṃ yathā bhavastathā bharet*
*na sadā mathanaṃ śastaṃ māse samācaret* (47)
*sadā rasanayā yogī mārgaṃ na parisaṃkramet*
*evaṃ dvādaśavarṣānte saṃsiddhirbhavati dhruvā* (48)
*śarīre sakalaṃ viśvaṃ paśyantyātmāvibhedataḥ*
*brahmāṇḍo 'yaṃ mahāmārgo rājadantordhvakuṇḍalī* (49)

**Anvay**

*niyojya*: having attached to; *śalākikām*: thin rod; *svarnajām*: made of gold; *raupyajām*: made of silver; *vā api*: or even; *lohajām*: made of iron; *nāsikārandhram*: nostrils; *tantunā*: by means of a thread; *siktena dugdha*: impregnated with milk; *prāṇāt-nirudhya*: holding the breath; *hṛdaye*: in the heart;

*ātmanaḥ*: self; *sukham-āsanam*: comfortable position; *nyasya*: focusing; *cakṣuṣī*: eyes; *bhrūmadhye*: on the eyebrow centre; *śanaiḥ*: slowly; *kuryāt*: one should perform; *sumathanam*: auspicious mathana; *ṣaṇmāsam*: in six months; *mathana-avasthā*: state of mathana; *prajāyate bhāvena*: comes naturally; *yathā*: just like; *suṣuptiḥ-bālānām*: sleep of children; *bharet*: is maintained; *samācaret*: one should practise; *na sadā*: not always; *śastam mathanam*: excellent mathana; *māse*: [every] month; *yogī*: yogin; *na sadā parisaṃkramet*: should not always revolve; *rasanayā*: tongue; *margam*: path; *dvādaśa-varṣānte*: after twelve years; *bhavati dhruvā*: there is sure; *saṃsiddhiḥ*: attainment of siddhis; *sakalam viśvam*: whole universe; *paśyanti*: is seen; *śarīre*: in the body; *ātmā-vibhedataḥ*: not distinct from the ātman; *ayam mahā-mārgaḥ*: this great path; *ūrdhvakuṇḍalī*: ascending kuṇḍalīni; *rājadanta*: infinite ruler; *brahmandaḥ*: cosmos.

**Translation**

Having attached a thin rod made of gold, silver or even iron to the nostrils by means of a thread impregnated with milk, holding the breath in the heart, the self [in] a comfortable position [and] focusing the eyes on the eyebrow centre, one should slowly perform the auspicious mathana. In six months, the state of mathana comes naturally, just like the state of sleep in children is maintained. One should not always practise [this] excellent mathana [every] month. The yogin should not always revolve his tongue [on] the path. After twelve years there is sure [to be] attainment of siddhis. The whole universe is seen in the body [as] indistinct from the ātman. This great path [of] ascending kuṇḍalīni is the infinite ruler [of] the cosmos.

**Commentary**

The practice of *sūtra neti*, cleansing the nostrils with a thread, is described here, as an adjunct to khecarī mudrā. Sūtra neti will help to rebalance and open the pranic pathways of iḍā and piṅgalā, removing any obstruction of air or prāṇa in these flows. The left nostril corresponds to the physical termination point of iḍā nāḍī, and the right nostril to the physical termination of piṅgalā nāḍī. Iḍā controls the mental energy and piṅgalā the vital. When these two major channels are in equilibrium, the third and most important channel, suṣumnā, which controls the spiritual force, opens. Without the opening of suṣumnā, the highest stage of khecarī, described above, is impossible to attain.

**Technique**

*Stage one, preparing the sūtra:* Cut a length of silken thread, about one and a half meters long, to be used for the practice. Attach a thin rod made of gold, silver, or iron, at the midpoint of the thread. Heat some beeswax in a spoon, over a flame, and apply it to one end of the thread. Allow the wax to dry and harden. Soak the thread just below the beeswax, along with the attached rod, in a bowl of milk for a few minutes, before beginning the practice of sūtra neti.

*Stage two, awareness of body and breath:* Sit in a comfortable meditation position. The bowl of milk, with the thread soaking in it, should be placed in front of you. Allow the entire body to relax in the posture from head to toe. Leave all worries and concerns, regarding the daily life, and draw the attention within. Focus the awareness on the breath. Practice slow rhythmic breathing. Inhale slowly from the nostrils down to the heart. Hold the breath at the heart for a comfortable duration. Exhale slowly from the heart back upward to the nostrils. Establish a comfortable rhythm of the breath, while inhaling, holding and exhaling.

*Stage three, inserting the thread:* Change back to normal breathing. Pick up the end of the thread with the beeswax from the bowl in front of you. Slowly begin to insert it into the opening of the right nostril. Push the thread upward into the right nostril and into the opening at the back of the throat.

Manoeuvre the thread, so that it passes down the throat. Then pull it out manually from the back of the throat through the mouth.

*Stage four, pulling the thread:* Hold the two ends of the thread. The left hand holds the thread coming from the mouth, and the right hand holds the thread from the nostrils. Practise *śambhavi mudrā,* holding the gaze inward at the eyebrow centre. Resume the awareness of the breath. Inhale slowly downward from the nostrils to the heart. Hold the breath at the heart and simultaneously pull the thread up and down, so that the rod massages the entire length of the right nostril. This is called mathana. Rotate the thread with the rod affixed up and down the right nostril slowly from three to five times. Then exhale slowly back upward from the heart to the nostrils. This is one round. Practise four more rounds. Then withdraw the thread from the right nostril, and perform the practice in the same way through the left nostril for five rounds.

*Stage five, alternative method:* You can also insert the thread up the right nostril and pull it out through the left nostril. Hold the two ends of the thread, with the right end from the right nostril in the right hand, and the left end from the left nostril in the left hand. Focus the gaze at the eyebrow centre and resume the heart breath, as described above. Perform five rounds of mathana in this way, so that the rod massages the right nostril. Then remove the thread. Insert the thread up the left nostril and pull it out through the right. Perform five rounds of mathana in this way.

*Stage six, spontaneous mathana:* In six months the state of mathana comes naturally and is maintained, like the state of sleep in children. This continuous state of mathana allows the flow of iḍā and piṅgalā to remain equalised and keeps suṣumnā open for longer durations of time. This is the condition required for the last stage of khecarī to be successful.

*Precautions:* However, the text further states that the yogi should not practise this auspicious mathana every month. There must be a break for the preservation of the vital and mental forces. The channel of suṣumnā should not remain open all the time. Similarly, the yogi should not practise khecarī, revolving the tongue on the path of suṣumnā, for continuous durations of time.

*Benefits:* The yogi who is able to maintain this practice for twelve years will surely attain siddhi, the powers of perfection. He will experience the whole universe as ātman, the pure self, within the body. The path of *ūrdhva*, the ascending, kuṇḍalinī is the infinite ruler of the universe. It is she who creates all existence while descending, who maintains the creation while resting at its base, and who dissolves all creation back into her cosmic being while ascending.

इति द्वीतीयोऽध्यायः ।।

*iti dvītīyo 'dhyāyaḥ*

Thus [ends] the second chapter.

# Chapter Three
## तृतियोऽध्यायः
## *tṛtiyo 'dhyāyaḥ*

मेलनमनु: । हीं भं सं पं फं सं क्षं ।
*melanamanuḥ*: *hīṃ bhaṃ saṃ paṃ phaṃ saṃ kshaṃ*

पद्मज उवाच ।
*padmaja uvāca*
The Lotus-born said:

### Verses 1 and 2: Auspicious days

अमावास्या च प्रतिपत्पौर्णमासी च शंकर ।
अस्याः का वर्ण्यते संज्ञा एतदाख्याहि तत्त्वतः ।।१।।
प्रतिपद्दिनती 'काले अमावास्या तथैव च ।
पौर्णमास्यां स्थिरीकुर्यात्स च पन्था हि नान्यथा ।।२।।

*amāvāsyā ca pratipatpaurṇamāsī ca śaṅkara*
*asyāḥ kā varṇyate saṃjñā etadākhyāhi tattvataḥ* (1)
*pratipaddinatī 'kāle amāvāsyā tathaiva ca*
*paurṇamāsyāṃ sthirīkuryātsa ca panthā hi nānyathā* (2)

**Anvay**
*śaṅkara*: o Śaṅkara; *kā*: which one; *amāvāsyā*: night of the dark moon; *ca*: or; *pratipatpaurṇamāsī*: beginning of the full moon; *varṇyate*: is described as; *asyāḥ saṃjñā*: its sign; *etad*: this; *tattvataḥ*: truly; *ākhyā*: name; *sthirī-kuryāt*: it should be established; *akāle*: when is not the right time; *pratipaddinatī*: first day of the lunar fortnight; *tathaiva ca*: or; *amāvāsyā*: night of the new moon; *paurṇamāsyām*: day of the full moon; *sā panthā*: this [is] the way; *ca nānyathā*: and no other.

**Translation**
O Śaṅkara, which one, the night of the dark moon or the beginning of the full moon, is described as its sign? This [is] truly [its] name. It should be established when is not the right time: the first day of the lunar fortnight, or the night of the dark moon, or the day of the full moon. This [is] the way, and no other.

**Commentary**
The lunar calendar was used in ancient times and is still consulted today to determine the best dates for initiating auspicious practices or conducting events. The lunar calendar is based upon the monthly cycles of the phases of the moon, in contrast to the solar calendar, which is based upon the solar year. The lunar month is comprised of 29 days. The days of the lunar calendar are called *tithi*. Each month has two cycles: 14 days waxing or *śukla pakṣa*, bright fortnight, and 14 days waning or *kṛṣṇa pakṣa*, dark fortnight, plus a few hours extra in-between to make up the 29 days. There are twelve lunar cycles in one year.

Within these two cycles that occur each month, several days are considered to be auspicious. The three days generally observed are referred to in the verses above. The full moon day, or *pūrṇima*, occurs at the end of the waxing cycle. This day is very powerful, and can be appreciated by all. But little is generally known about the dark moon, or *amāvāsyā,* which is the second auspicious day. The dark moon day occurs at the end of the waning cycle, before the beginning of the waxing cycle, when there is no conjunction between the sun and the moon. Therefore, the moon is not visible at all during this time. The next lunar month begins on the day of the new moon, *pratipaddinatī*, when the moon comes into conjunction with the sun again, and this is the third auspicious day.

The question is asked here: which of these days is described as its sign, the dark moon day or the first day of the new moon? These two days are often described as one and the same, although they are actually distinct from one another with their own attributes. It is also asked, when is it not the right time to initiate an event or a sādhana, on the dark moon day, the new moon day, or the full moon day? Generally, the dark moon day is auspicious for starting tantric or esoteric practices. The new moon day is beneficial for starting sādhanas of a universal nature. The full moon day is conducive for conducting ceremonies and public worship.

## Verses 3 and 4a: Renunciation

कामेन विषयाकाङ्क्षी विषयात्काममोहितः ।

द्वावेव संत्यजेन्नित्यं निरञ्जनमुपाश्रयेत् ।।३।।

अपरं संत्यजेत्सर्वं यदिच्छेदात्मनो हितम् ।४।

*kāmena viṣayākāṅkṣī viṣayātkāmamohitaḥ*
*dvāveva saṃtyajennityaṃ nirañjanamupāśrayet* (3)
*aparaṃ saṃtyajetsarvaṃ yadicchedātmano hitam* (4a)

**Anvay**

*kāṅkṣī*: longing for; *viṣayā*: sensual enjoyment; *kāmena*: because of desire; *mohitaḥ*: one is deluded by; *viṣayāt-kāma*: desire for sensual enjoyment; *saṃtyajet*: one should renounce; *dvau*: two; *nityam*: forever; *upāśrayet*: one should devote oneself to; *niranjanam*: that which is stainless; *aparam*: moreover; *saṃtyajet*: one should abandon; *sarvam hitam*: everything pleasurable; *yad icchet*: which one wishes; *ātmanaḥ*: for oneself.

**Translation**

[When there is] longing for sensual enjoyment because of desire, one is deluded by the desire for sensual enjoyment. One should renounce [these] two [and] forever devote oneself to that which is stainless. Moreover, one should abandon everything pleasurable, which one wishes for oneself.

**Commentary**

Whenever there is longing for sensual enjoyment, the mind always becomes clouded by that desire. Longing and desire for sensual experience create endless waves in the mind, which aggravate and disturb it, making sādhana impossible. The longing will continue on in the mind, long after the practice is over, causing tumult and unrest, until it is fulfilled. Even after satisfying the desire, however, there is no respite, for another desire will immediately replace it. Hence, desire, longing and satisfaction form a continual cycle, which bind one to the world. There can be no liberation in this life for one whose mind is set upon following desires.

Therefore, the yogi who wishes to dedicate himself to a regular practice must first free the mind of all hankering and longing for external things. The sādhaka must develop sensory control to such a degree that as soon as the thoughts start to wander into areas of desire, he or she is able to bring it back immediately and focus on the practice at hand and the inner goal to be achieved. There must be a clear distinction between sensory satisfaction and self realisation. One must be determined to sacrifice the former in order to achieve the latter.

The yogi must be prepared to renounce desire and longing for sensory experience forever, in order to devote himself completely to that which is stainless and permanent. There is no external person, place or object that can be considered absolutely pure. All material existence is impermanent and impure, because it is bound by the elements and influenced by time and space. What then can be considered stainless in this world? Only the pure consciousness, which is unbound and unaffected by the trammels of life.

Therefore, in order to become a yogi, one must abandon all pleasures, especially those which one wishes for oneself, and focus on attaining the absolute consciousness. It is interesting to note that the pleasures and welfare that one may wish or seek for others have a different effect on the mind. Wishing others well has a calming and expansive effect, generating love and good will all around. Even a renunciate should practise it in order to bring peace to the world. The fruits of sādhana may also be dedicated in this way for the happiness and welfare of all beings.

## Verses 4b to 7a: Manas and śakti

शक्तिमध्ये मनः कृत्वा मनः शक्तेश्च मध्यगम् ।।४।।

मनसा मन आलोक्य तत्यजेत्परं पदम् ।

मन एव हि बिन्दुश्च उत्पत्तिस्थितिकारणम् ।।५।।

मनसोत्पद्यते बिन्दुर्यथा क्षीरं घृतात्मकम् ।

न च बन्धनमध्यस्थं तद्वे कारणमानसम् ।।६।।

चन्द्रार्कमध्यमा शक्तिर्यत्रस्था तत्र बन्धनम् ।७।

*śaktimadhye manaḥ kṛtvā manaḥ śakteśca madhyagam* (4b)
*manasā mana ālokya tattyajetparaṃ padam*
*mana eva hi binduśca utpattisthitikāraṇam* (5)
*manasotpadyate binduryathā kṣīraṃ ghṛtātmakam*
*na ca bandhanamadhyasthaṃ tadve kāraṇamānasam* (6)
*candrārkamadhyamā śaktiryatrasthā tatra bandhanam* (7a)

**Anvay**

*kṛtvā*: having put; *manaḥ śaktimadhye*: *manas* within *śakti*; *manaḥ madhyagam śakteḥ*: manas being amongst śakti; *ca ālokya*: and viewed; *manaḥ manasā*: manas through manas; *tyajet*: one leaves; *tat param padam*: this highest stage; *hi*: for; *manaḥ eva binduḥ*: manas [is] indeed the *bindu*; *ca*: and; *kāraṇam*: cause; *utpatti-sthiti*: creation and continued existence; *binduḥ utpadyate manasā*: bindu comes into existence through manas; *yathā*: just as; *ghṛta-ātmakam*: ghee comes from; *kṣīram*: milk; *tat kāraṇa-mānasam*: its mental cause; *ve*: definitely; *na bandhana-madhya-stham*: not situated in the middle of bondage; *bandhanam tatra*: bondage [is] there; *yatra śaktiḥ sthā*: where śakti is located; *candra-arka-madhyamā*: between the moon and the sun.

**Translation**

Having put *manas* within *śakti*, manas being amongst śakti, and viewed manas through manas, one leaves this highest stage. For manas [is] indeed the *bindu*, and the cause [of] creation and continued existence. Bindu comes into existence through manas, just as ghee comes from milk. Its mental cause [is] definitely not situated in the middle of bondage. Binding [is] there where śakti is located between the moon and the sun.

**Commentary**

*Manas* and *śakti* are the two principles of creation. Here, manas refers to mind in the sense of consciousness, and śakti, the eternal energy. All existence evolves from these two. When manas functions from within śakti, there is creation and the different experiences of name and form and ideation. Oneself and the world around are seen from that perspective. However, when manas is withdrawn from śakti, ie., *puruṣa* is withdrawn from *prakṛti*, then all existence is seen as consciousness, manas within manas. All beings, all worlds, all existence are only consciousness. This is said to be the absolute truth; while the vision of manas within śakti is the relative.

Having viewed and understood these two perspectives: manas within śakti, and manas within manas, one leaves this highest stage of realisation. Individual being is imminent for all those who are born. *Bindu* is the point or source of manas, where being becomes manifest. So, manas is indeed bindu, the cause of creation and continued existence. Bindu comes into existence through manas. The point or source of being is thus an evolute of consciousness, in the same way that butter is an evolute of milk. The unmanifest, unbound consciousness undergoes a transformation at this point, whereby it becomes manifest and bound. Bindu is the entry point, where being becomes manifest, as well as the exit point, where all being is unmanifest, formless and timeless.

The cause of consciousness is definitely not any kind of binding, fettering or holding. Consciousness in itself is free from all bondage and limitation. The consciousness becomes bound only when it associates with śakti and manifests in-between the sun and moon, in the body and mind, and in the world of name and form.

## Verses 7b to 9a: Practice of kuṇḍalinī yoga

ज्ञात्वा सुषुम्नां तद्भेदं कृत्वा वायुं च मध्यगम् ।।७।।
स्थित्वासौवैन्दवस्थाने घ्राणरन्ध्रे निरोधयेत् ।
वायुं बिन्दुं समाख्यातं सत्त्वं प्रकृतिमेव च ।।८।।
षट् चक्राणि परिज्ञत्वा प्रविशेत्सुखमण्डलम् ।९।

*jñātvā suṣumnāṃ tadbhedaṃ kṛtvā vāyuṃ ca madhyagam* (7b)
*sthitvāsauvaindavasthāne ghrāṇarandhre nirodhayet*
*vāyuṃ binduṃ samākhyātaṃ sattvaṃ prakṛtimeva ca* (8)
*ṣaṭ cakrāṇi parijñatvā praviśetsukhamaṇḍalam* (9a)

**Anvay**

*jñātvā suṣumnām*: having known the suṣumnā; *tat-bhedam*: its *piercing*; *kṛtvā vāyum madhyagam*: moved the prāṇa up the centre; *ca sthitvā*: and remained; *aindava-sthāne*: in the site of the moon; *nirodhayet*: one should close; *ghrāṇarandhre*: nostrils; *parijñatvā*: having experienced; *vāyum*: prāṇa; *bindum samākhyātam*: bindu as described; *sattvam prakṛtim*: quality of *sattva*; *ca ṣaṭ cakrāṇi*: and the six cakras; *praviśet*: one enters; *sukha-maṇḍalam*: sphere of joy.

**Translation**

Having known the suṣumnā [and] its piercing, moved the prāṇa up the centre, and remained in the site of the moon, one should close the nostrils. Having experienced the prāṇa, the bindu as described, the quality of *sattva* and the six cakras, one enters the sphere of joy.

**Commentary**

Here the path of kuṇḍalinī yoga is succinctly described in a simple and easy formula:

*The first step* is to become aware of *suṣumnā nāḍī,* located at the centre of the spinal column, and its significance as the direct channel of the kuṇḍalinī śakti, both descending from spirit into matter and ascending from matter into spirit.

*The second step* is to open the suṣumnā by rotating the prāṇa along with the breath through the centre of this pathway. Inhale slowly upward from the base of suṣumnā at mūlādhāra cakra to bindu cakra at the top back of the head, and then exhale back down from bindu to mūlādhāra. Imagine particles of light or streaks of light flowing upward and downward with the breath. You may also experience heat or cold, itching or tingling along with this movement.

*The third step* is to become aware of the six major cakras and their locations alongside the suṣumnā. Imagine you are piercing each cakra in turn with the sharp needle of the prāṇa, with each ascending breath, and again with each descending breath.

*The fourth step* is to practise breath retention at bindu cakra, the site of the moon. While inhaling, rotate the breath and the prāṇa upward through the centre of suṣumnā from mūlādhāra to bindu, piercing each cakra in turn. Hold the breath at bindu for as long as you feel comfortable. Focus on a bright point of light there. Then exhale back down the suṣumnā from bindu to mūlādhāra, again piercing each cakra point in turn.

*The fifth step* comes after experiencing the movement of prāṇa in suṣumnā and breath retention at bindu, as described in the earlier stages. Sit quietly in a comfortable pose and meditate on the quality of *sattva*, in the form of stillness, luminosity and peace, until you enter the sphere of *ānanda*, bliss and joy absolute.

## Verses 9b to 13: Stairway to enlightenment

मूलाधार स्वाधिष्ठानं मणिपुरं तृतीयकम् ।।९।।
अनाहतं विशुद्धं च आज्ञाचक्रं च षष्ठकम् ।
आधारं गुदमित्युक्तं स्वाधिष्ठानं तु लैङ्गिकम् ।।१०।।
मणिपुरं नाभिदेशं हृदयस्थमनाहतम् ।
विशुद्धिः कण्ठमूले च आज्ञाचक्रं च मस्तकम् ।।११।।
षट् चक्राणि परिज्ञत्वा प्रविशेत्सुखमण्डले ।
प्रविशेद्वायुमाकृष्य तयैवोर्ध्वं नियोजयेत् ।।१२।।
एवं समभ्यसेद्वायुं स ब्रह्माण्डमयो भवेत् ।
वायुं बिन्दुं तथा चक्रं चित्तं चैव समभ्यसेत् ।।१३।।

*mūlādhāra svādhiṣṭhānaṃ maṇipuraṃ tṛtīyakam* (9b)
*anāhataṃ viśuddhaṃ ca ājñācakraṃ ca ṣaṣṭhakam*
*ādhāraṃ gudamityuktaṃ svādhiṣṭhānaṃ tu laiṅgikam* (10)
*maṇipuraṃ nābhideśaṃ hṛdayasthamanāhatam*
*viśuddhih kaṇṭhamūle ca ājñācakraṃ ca mastakam* (11)
*ṣaṭ cakrāṇi parijñatvā praviśetsukhamaṇḍale*
*praviśedvāyumākṛṣya tayaivordhvaṃ niyojayet* (12)
*evaṃ samabhyasedvāyuṃ sa brahmāṇḍamayo bhavet*
*vāyuṃ binduṃ tathā cakraṃ cittaṃ caiva samabhyaset* (13)

**Anvay**

*mūlādhāra*: mūlādhāra cakra; *svādhiṣṭhānam*: svādhiṣṭhāna; *maṇipuram*: manipura; *tṛtīyakam*: third; *anāhatam*: anāhata; *viśuddham*: viśuddhi; *ca*: and; *ājñā*: ājñā; *ṣaṣṭhakam*: sixth; *iti uktam*: it is said; *ādhāram*: base; *gudam*: anus; *laingikam*: sexual; *nābhi-deśam*: area of the navel; *hṛdayastham*: placed in the heart; *viśuddhiḥ kaṇṭha-mūle*: viśuddhi at the base of the throat; *ca ājñā-cakram mastakam*: and ājñā cakra in the skull; *parijñatvā*: having experienced; *ṣaṭ cakrāṇi*: six cakras; *praviśet*: one enters; *sukha-maṇḍale*: sphere of joy; *vāyum-ākṛṣya*: having drawn in the breath or prāṇa; *niyojayet*: one should direct; *taya ūrdhvam*: it upwards; *sa bhavet*: he becomes; *brahmāṇḍamayaḥ*: part of the cosmos; *samabhyaset-vāyum evam*: practises this breath control; *tathā*: therefore; *samabhyaset*: one should practise; *vāyum bindum cakram ca cittam*: vāyu, bindu, cakras and *citta.*

**Translation**

[They are] *mūlādhāra, svādhiṣṭhāna, maṇipura* the third, *anāhata, viśuddhi,* and *ājñā,* the sixth. It is said the base [cakra is] in the anus, svādhiṣṭhāna in the sexual [region], maṇipura in the area of the navel, anāhata is placed in the heart, viśuddhi at the base of the throat, and ājñā cakra in the skull. Having experienced the six cakras, one enters the sphere of joy. Having drawn in the vāyu, one should direct [it] upwards. He becomes part of the cosmos [who] practises this breath control. Therefore one should practise [control of] vāyu, bindu, cakras and *citta.*

**Commentary**

These verses further elucidate the pathway of kuṇḍalinī yoga. The principle philosophy and practices of kuṇḍalinī yoga deal with the cakras, the psychic energy centers located alongside suṣumnā. The six cakras, along with their locations, are given here, as follows: (i) mūlādhāra at the anus or perineum, (ii) svādhiṣṭhāna in the pubic region, (iii) maṇipura at the navel region, (iv) anāhata at the heart, (v) viśuddhi at the base of the throat, and (vi) ājñā in the skull, at the mid-brain. Having experienced the six cakras, one enters the sphere of joy.

## Verses 14 to 18a: Significance of yoga, guru and sādhana

समाधिमेकेन सममममृतं यान्ति योगिनः ।

यथाग्निर्दारुमध्यस्थो नोत्तिष्ठेन्मथनं विना ॥१४॥

विना चाभ्यासयोगेन जञानदीपस्तथा न हि ।

घटमध्यगतो दीपो बाह्ये नैव प्रकाशते ॥१५॥

भिन्ने तस्मिन्घटे चैव दीपज्वाला च भासते ।

स्वकायं घटमित्युक्तं यथा दीपो हि तत्पदम् ॥१६॥

गुरुवाक्यसमाभिन्ने ब्रह्मज्ञानं स्फुटीभवेत् ।

कर्णधारं गुरुं प्राप्य कृत्वा सूक्ष्मं तरन्ति च ॥१७॥

अभ्यासवासनाशक्त्या तरन्ति भवसागरम् ।१८।

*samādhimekena samamamṛtaṃ yānti yoginaḥ*
*yathāgnirdārumadhyastho nottiṣṭhenmathanaṃ vinā* (14)
*vinā cābhyāsayogena jñānadīpastathā na hi*
*ghaṭamadhyagato dīpo bāhye naiva prakāśate* (15)
*bhinne tasminghaṭe caiva dīpajvālā ca bhāsate*
*svakāyaṃ ghaṭamityuktaṃ yathā dīpo hi tatpadam* (16)
*guruvākyasamābhinne brahmajñānaṃ sphuṭībhavet*
*karṇadhāraṃ guruṃ prāpya kṛtvā sūkṣmaṃ taranti ca* (17)
*abhyāsavāsanāśaktyā taranti bhavasāgaram* (18a)

**Anvay**

*yoginaḥ yānti*: yogins attain; *samam-amṛtam*: pure nectar of immortality; *samādhim-ekena*: through *samādhi* alone; *yathā*: just as; *agniḥ*: fire; *madhya-sthaḥ*: inherent in; *dāru*: timber; *na uttiṣṭhet*: does not rise up; *vinā mathanam*: without friction; *tathā*: so; *jñāna-dīpaḥ*: light of wisdom; *na*: not; *vinā abhyāsa-yogena*: without the practice of yoga; *dīpaḥ*:light; *ghaṭa-madhyagataḥ*: inside a pot; *na prakāśate*: does not shine; *bāhye*: outside; *eva*: only; *tasmin-ghaṭe bhinne*: when the pot is broken; *dīpa-jvālā*: flame of light; *bhāsate*: is visible; *iti*: thus; *sva-kāyam*: one's body; *uktam*:

is spoken of as; *ghaṭam*: vessel; *yathā*: while; *tat-padam*: its cause; *dīpaḥ*: light; *samābhinne*: when it is completely broken; *guru-vākya*: by the speech of the guru; *brahma-jñānam*: divine wisdom of Brahma; *bhavet*: becomes; *sphuṭī*: clear; *prāpya*: having attained; *kṛtvā*: made; *gurum karṇadhāram*: guru the helmsman; *taranti*: one crosses; *sūkṣmam*: subtle dimension; *ca*: and; *bhavasāgaram*: ocean of worldly existence; *śaktyā*: through the power; *vāsanā*: desire for; *abhyāsa*: sādhana.

**Translation**

Yogins attain the pure nectar of immortality through *samādhi* alone. Just as the fire inherent in timber does not rise up without friction, so the light of wisdom does not [appear] without the practice of yoga. The light inside a pot does not shine outside. Only when the pot is broken, does the flame of light become visible. Thus, one's body is spoken of as the vessel, while its cause [is] light. When it is completely broken by the speech of the guru, the divine wisdom of Brahma becomes clear. Having attained [it and] made the guru the helmsman, one crosses the subtle dimension and the ocean of worldly existence through the power [of] the desire for sādhana.

**Commentary**

The pure nectar of immortality has been sought by renunciates, mystics and seekers of all traditions worldwide for millennia, perhaps even from the beginning of civilisation. But very few have had a clear notion of what this nectar actually is, and where it is to be found. Kuṇḍalinī yoga is a very ancient science, belonging to the early tantras. Here, we can find the answer to these questions in the concept of the kuṇḍalinī and its entry point into the material dimension at bindu cakra. The principle of creation was explained in this way by the ancient seers.

When the kuṇḍalinī śakti enters the point at bindu, she

unleashes the flow of life in the form of a powerful fluid, called *amṛta*, or immortal nectar. This amṛta is the source of eternal life and, at bindu, it remains indestructible. However, as the nectar falls down from bindu into the lower centers, its quality and propensity changes. From viśuddhi cakra, behind the throat, the nectar becomes activated with *viṣ*, the principle of degeneration, which is responsible for incurring disease, old age and death.

As the nectar of life drips down further from viśuddhi into the lower cakras, it is used up by the systems of the body, as well as the external activities and associations, which the body engages with. In order to control this downward process of dissipation and degeneration, it is necessary to redirect the nectar, so that it merges back into the field of consciousness above viśuddhi. Through the practices of kuṇḍalinī yoga, yogis were able to attain *samādhi*, the transcendental state of consciousness, by raising the kuṇḍalinī and establishing the nectar in the higher centers.

When the kuṇḍalinī force ascends through the cakras, it draws the nectar back upward along with it. Hence, the mind and perception become finer and subtler with each cakra that the kuṇḍalinī passes through. This results in an ongoing flow of wisdom and subtle perception, which the yogi is able to access freely. In the same way that the fire inherent in wood will only arise when adequate friction is applied, similarly the light of wisdom will only appear in a person through the practice of yoga. Today, yoga is regarded as a form of physical exercise. But the yogis of old regarded it as a means to kindle the light within and thereby attain self-realisation.

The light inside a fire pot does not shine outside. The flame of light only becomes visible outside, when the pot is broken. In this way, the physical body is compared to the pot, but its cause is the light, burning within. When the illusion of the pot, the identity with the body, is completely broken by the teachings of the guru, the divine wisdom of Brahman, the ever expanding consciousness, becomes clear. Guru is spoken of as 'he who removes the darkness'. Guru is thus the illumined one, for only light can remove darkness.

Having attained this wisdom, and made the guru his helmsman, the yogi crosses the ocean of worldly existence and also the subtle existence, through the power of and the desire for *sādhana*. Yoga is a vast body of systems and practices, which can be applied by different persons at different times and in different situations. Sādhana, on the other hand, is a specific formula of practices, which will help the yogi to attain his or her particular goals.

Learning yoga is one stage and teaching yoga is another. But to maintain a regular yoga practice, over a long period of time, with firm faith and conviction, until one's goals are achieved, is sādhana. In the absence of sādhana, very little can be attained through the practice of yoga, even though one may study all the principles and practices. At the end of the day, an ounce of sādhana is better than a ton of theory. In order to maintain a regular sādhana, one must have a disciplined lifestyle and a very powerful desire to attain self-realisation. This desire must be more important than the achievement of any worldly desire, status or aim.

Drawing in the breath and prāṇa, one should direct it upwards through the suṣumnā pathway. By practising this form of breath control, the consciousness is expanded and one becomes part of the cosmos. Otherwise, while breathing normally, the mind is drawn outside, together with the senses, and engages with the external affairs of the world. Therefore, one should practise control of vāyu (breath), bindu (point at top back of the head), cakras (psychic energy centres) and citta (mind and consciousness). This is the pathway to enlightenment, and no other.

## Verses 18b to 21a: Evolution of sound and Soham

परायामङ्कुरीभूया पश्यन्त्यां द्विदलीकृता ।।१८।।

मध्यमायां मुकुलिता वैखर्यां विकसीकृता ।

पूर्वं यथोदिता या वाग्विलोमेनास्तगा भवेत् ।।१९।।

तस्या वाचः परो देवः कूटस्थो वाक्प्रबोधकः ।

सोहमस्मीति निश्चित्य यः सदा वर्तते पुमान् ।।२०।।

शब्दैरुच्चावचैर्नीचैर्भाषितोऽपि न लिप्यते ।२१।

*parāyāmaṅkurībhūyā paśyantyāṃ dvidalīkṛtā* (18b)
*madhyamāyāṃ mukulitā vaikharyāṃ vikasīkṛtā*
*pūrvaṃ yathoditā yā vāgvilomenāstagā bhavet* (19)
*tasyā vācaḥ paro devaḥ kūṭastho vākprabodhakaḥ*
*sohamasmīti niścitya yaḥ sadā vartate pumān* (20)
*śabdairuccāvacairnīcairbhāṣito 'pi na lipyate* (21a)

**Anvay**

*yā pūrvam uditā*: that aforesaid; *aṅkurībhūyā*: sprouts; *parāyām*: in *para*; *dvidalī-kṛtā*: makes two leaves; *paśyantyām*: in *paśyanti*; *mukulitā*: buds; *madhyamāyām*: in *madhyama*; *vikasīkṛtā*: blossoms; *vaikharyām*: in *vaikhari*; *bhavet astagā*: becomes set; *vilomena*: by reversing this order; *paraḥ devaḥ*: Supreme Divinity; *kūṭa-sthaḥ*: is at the peak; *vācaḥ*: of *vāc*; *yaḥ pumān*: whoever; *vartate*: remains; *sadā*: always; *niścitya*: convinced; *iti 'soham asmi'*: that 'I am Soham'; *vāc-prabodhakaḥ*: causes the *vāc* to blossom; *na api*: not even; *lipyate*: is affected by; *uccāvacaiḥ-nīcaiḥ-śabdaiḥ*: by various vile words; *bhāṣitaḥ*: are spoken.

**Translation**

That aforesaid [*vāc*], [which] sprouts in *para*, makes two leaves in *paśyanti,* buds in *madhyama* [and] blossoms in *vaikhari*, becomes set by reversing this order. The supreme divinity is at the peak of *vāc.* Whoever remains always convinced that '*I am Soham'*, causes the *vāc* to blossom [and] is not even affected by various vile words [that] are spoken.

**Commentary**

According to yoga philosophy, sound is the first principle of creation. In the Bible it also says, 'In the beginning was the word, and the word was with God, and the word was God.' The first sound vibration to sprout in the supreme consciousness is known as *para vāc.* This is the subtlest sound that gives rise to all of creation. This pure sound produces two shoots. In *paśyanti,* or mental sound, which reverberates in the mind, as we think, feel, remember, and dream, it buds. In *madhyama,* the sound midway between inside and outside, neither mental nor audible, which arises while whispering, it blossoms. From madhyama, *vaikari,* or audible sound, arises. In vaikari, the sound vibration becomes set and then the order is reversed, i.e. from vaikari, madhyama arises, from madhyama paśyanti, and from paśyanti, para. In this way, the entire creation goes on manifesting and dissolving itself throughout eternity.

The supreme divinity, which we may call God, or cosmic consciousness, is the ultimate source of vac. Whoever repeats the sound *Soham asmi*, I am Soham, or I am That (supreme consciousness), with firm faith in this truth, causes the vāc or sound vibration to blossom. By hearing, thinking or repeating this particular sound vibration, it becomes very powerful, effecting the entire field of the person, as well as the environment all around. The field of sound vibration pervades and sustains all existence. Altering the sound vibration in any given object, person or place, causes changes to occur on all dimensions within and around it. This is the power of sound. Therefore, sound vibration may be utilised to create as well as to destroy, to protect as well as to harm. One who repeats this sound and always remains convinced that 'I am Soham' remains unaffected by the situations and conditions of life, even by various vile words that are spoken.

## Verses 21b to 26: Meditation on the ātman

विश्वश्च तैजसश्चैव प्राज्ञश्चेति च ते त्रयः ।।२१।।
विराड्ढिरण्यगर्भश्च ईश्वरश्चेति ते त्रयः ।
ब्रह्माण्डं चैव पिण्डाण्दं लोका भूरादयः क्रमात् ।।२२।।
स्वस्वोपाधिलयादेव लीयन्ते प्रत्यगात्मनि ।
अण्डं ज्ञानाग्निना तप्तं लीयते कारणैः सह ।।२३।।
परमात्मनि लीनं तत्परं ब्रह्मैव जायते ।
ततः स्तिमितगम्भीरं तेजो न तमस्ततम् ।।२४।।
अनाख्यमनभिव्यक्तं सत्किंचिदवशिष्यते ।
ध्यात्वा मध्यस्थमात्मानं कलसान्तरदीपवत् ।।२५।।
अङ्गुष्ठमात्रमात्मानमधूमज्योतिरूपकम् ।
प्रकाशयन्तमन्तस्स्थं ध्यायेत्कूटस्थमव्ययम् ।।२६।।

*viśvaśca taijasaścaiva prājñaśceti ca te trayaḥ* (21b)
*virāḍḍhiraṇyagarbhaśca īśvaraśceti te trayaḥ*
*brahmāṅḍaṃ caiva piṇḍāṇdaṃ lokā bhūrādayaḥ kramāt* (22)
*svasvopādhilayādeva līyante pratyagātmani*
*aṇḍaṃ jñānāgninā taptaṃ līyate kāraṇaiḥ saha* (23)
*paramātmani līnaṃ tatparaṃ brahmaiva jāyate*
*tataḥ stimitagambhīraṃ tejo na tamastatam* (24)
*anākhyamanabhivyaktaṃ satkiṃcidavaśiṣyate*
*dhyātvā madhyasthamātmānaṃ kalasāntaradīpavat* (25)
*aṅguṣṭhamātramātmānamadhūmajyotirūpakam*
*prakāśayantamantassthaṃ dhyāyetkūṭasthamavyayam* (26)

**Anvay**

*te trayaḥ*: the three; *viśvaḥ*: waking; *taijasaḥ*: dreaming; *ca*: and; *prājñaḥ*: deep sleep; *ca te trayaḥ*: and the three; *virāt*: entire manifest universe; *hiraṇyagarbhaḥ*: cosmic subtle body; *ca īśvaraḥ*: supreme consciousness; *brahmāṅḍam*: macrocosm; *ca eva piṇḍāṇdam*: and even the microcosm;

*lokāḥ*: worlds; *bhūḥ-ādayaḥ*: earth and others; *layāt*: through absorption in; *svasva-upādhi*: their true attributes; *līyante*: are merged; *pratyagātmani*: into the inner self; *aṇḍam*: egg; *taptam*: heated; *jñāna-agninā*: by the fire of knowledge; *līyate*: is absorbed; *saha kāraṇaiḥ*: with its cause; *paramātmani*: into the supreme self; *jāyate līnam*: becomes merged in; *param brahma*: supreme Brahma; *tataḥ*: then; *stimita-gambhīram*: still and deep; *tejaḥ na tamaḥ*: light nor darkness; *anākhyam*: neither describable; *anabhivyaktam*: nor distinct; *dhyātvā*: reflect on; *madhya-stham-ātmānam*: *ātman* resting within the body; *dīpavat*: like a light; *kala-antara*: inside a jar; *kiṃcit*: just; *sat*: essence; *avaśiṣyate*: remains; *dhyāyet ātmānam*: one should think of *ātman*; *aṅguṣṭha-mātram*: size of a thumb; *jyoti-rūpakam*: form of light; *adhūma*: without smoke; *prakāśayantam-antaḥ-stham*: shining within; *kūṭastham-avyayam*: unchangeable and imperishable.

**Translation**

The three [states of consciousness]: waking, dreaming and deep sleep; and the three [aspects of existence]: the entire manifest universe, the cosmic subtle body and the supreme consciousness; the macrocosm and even the microcosm, the worlds of the earth and others, [all these], through absorption in their true attributes, are merged into the inner self. The egg, heated by the fire of knowledge, is absorbed with its cause into the supreme self [and] becomes merged in the supreme Brahma. Then, still and deep, [it is neither] light nor darkness, neither describable nor distinct. Reflect on the ātman resting within the body, like a light inside a jar. Just the essence remains. One should think of the ātman [as] the size of a thumb, a form of light, without smoke, shining within, unchangeable and imperishable.

**Commentary**

Just as sound is the underlying principle of creation, consciousness is the essence of existence. All beings, whether sentient or insentient, manifest or unmanifest, are bound together by consciousness. Ultimately, all existence is a part of the same consciousness. Although consciousness is one field, it can be experienced as three states: waking, dreaming and deep sleep. While awake, we become conscious of the world around us through the mind and senses. While dreaming, we experience the subconscious, and its inner manifestations. In deep sleep, we float in the unconscious, beyond all vestige of perception, ideation and dream. In this way, the one field is interwoven throughout the three states is consciousness. Similarly, consciousness is the one reality that pervades the three dimensions of existence: the manifest creation, the subtle cosmic cause, or womb of creation, and the supreme consciousness.

The macrocosm and the microcosm, the *lokas*, or planes of existence, the earth and others, all merge with the inner self by means of absorption into their true attribute, which is consciousness. The cosmic egg, or womb of creation, heated by the fire of *jñāna*, knowledge, is absorbed into its cause, *paramātman*, the supreme self, and merges into the *parambrahman*, the supreme, ever expanding consciousness. This consciousness is constant and steady, still and deep. It is neither light nor dark, distinct nor describable. Meditate on your own ātman, the pure consciousness, resting in the body, like a light inside a jar, until just the essence remains. Think of the atman as the size of your thumb. See or imagine it as a form of light, without any emanation of smoke, shining within. Unchangeable, imperishable and eternal.

## Verses 27 to 29: Spontaneous practice of jñāna yoga

विज्ञानात्मा तथा देहे जाग्रत्स्वप्नसुषुप्तितः ।

मायया मोहितः पश्चाद्बहुजन्मान्तरे पुनः ।।२७।।

सत्कर्मपरिपाकात्तु स्वविकारं चिकीर्षति ।

कोऽहं कथमयं दोषः संसाराख्य उपागतः ।।२८।।

जाग्रत्स्वप्ने व्यवहरन्त्सुषुप्तौ क्व गतिर्मम ।

इति चिन्तापरो भूत्वा स्वभासा च विशेषतः ।।२९।।

*vijñānātmā tathā dehe jāgratsvapnasuṣuptitaḥ*
*māyayā mohitaḥ paścādbahujanmāntare punaḥ* (27)
*satkarmaparipākāttu svavikāraṃ cikīrṣati*
*ko 'ham kathamayaṃ doṣaḥ saṃsārākhya upāgataḥ* (28)
*jāgratsvapne vyavaharantsuṣuptau kva gatirmama*
*iti cintāparo bhūtvā svabhāsā ca viśeṣataḥ* (29)

### Anvay

*vijñāna-ātmā*: *vijñāna ātman*; *dehe*: in the body; *mohitaḥ*: is deluded; *māyayā*: by the unreal; *jāgrat-svapna-suṣuptitaḥ*: waking, dreaming and sleeping; *paścāt*: at last; *bahu-janma-antare punaḥ*: after many births; *paripākāt*: as a result of; *sat-karma*: good karma; *cikīrṣati*: it wishes to return to; *sva-vikāram*: its true state; *kaḥ aham*: who am I?; *katham*: how; *ayam doṣaḥ*: this disease; *saṃsāra-akhya*: called *saṃsāra*; *upāgataḥ*: did come to; *kva gatiḥ*: what happens; *suṣuptau*: during deep sleep; *mama*: to me; *vyavaharant*: who is active in mundane life; *jāgrat-svapne*: in waking and dreaming; *iti*: it asks; *bhūtvā*: having become; *svabhāsā*: through its own light; *viśeṣataḥ*: above all; *cintāparaḥ*: engrossed in reflection.

### Translation

The *vijñāna ātman* in the body is deluded by the unreal [during the states of] waking, dreaming and sleeping. At last, after many births, as a result of good karma, it wishes to return to its true state. Who am I? How did this disease called *samsāra* come to [me]? What happens during deep sleep to me, who is active in mundane life in [the states of] waking and dreaming? It asks, having become engrossed in reflection through its own light, above all.

**Commentary**

The ātman is the pure self, or unbound consciousness. The *jīvātman* is the pure self, living in the body, and thus bound by it. The *vijñāna ātman* is the psychic or reflected knowledge of the jīvātman, which is limited by the states of waking, dreaming and sleeping. It is also influenced by the seed karmas or impressions of the associations derived from interactions with the world outside. Due to its proximity with the ātman, or pure self, the vijñāna ātman has the ability to discriminate between the real and the unreal. When focussed downward, however, it becomes identified with the mind and body, and is therefore deluded by the transitory nature of life, believing it to be permanent and real.

In this way, the ātman passes through many births and has many different experiences in life. At last, as a result of good karma and the fulfilment of residual desires, it wishes to return to its true nature, which is free from duality, limitation and identification. When this resolution dawns, the vijñāna ātman becomes dissatisfied with the worldly roles and associations, and begins to question itself and its existence. Through a process of inner analysis and reflection, it asks: Who am I? How did this disease called *samsāra,* worldly life, come upon me? What happens to me, where do I go, during deep sleep? In mundane life, who is active in the state of waking, and again, who is dreaming? Withdrawing the mind and senses, the vijñāna ātman becomes engrossed in meditation, and asks these questions through its own light, received from the pure ātman above it.

The upaniṣads are a body of ancient knowledge, which contain the experiences of rishis and seers of the vedic traditions, as well as some munis from traditions, such as yoga and tantra. Therefore, although this text is devoted to the teachings of kuṇḍalinī yoga, we find the vedantic approach, along with its practice of jñāna yoga, is also honored. According to vedānta, Brahman, the pure, ever-expanding consciousness, is the one absolute reality; everything else is illusion. However, according to yoga and tantra, this pure state of consciousness can only be attained by the awakening of kuṇḍalinī śakti. Without the awakening of energy, the highest consciousness remains obscure and remote. Therefore, in the yoga upaniṣads, we find the melding of traditions: yoga and tantra to awaken the energy followed by vedānta to realise the highest consciousness.

### Verses 30 to 32: Merging with the ātman

अज्ञानात्तु चिदाभासो बहिस्तापेन तापितः ।
दग्धं भवत्येव तदा तूलपिण्डमिवाग्निना ॥३०॥
दहरस्थः प्रत्यगात्मा नष्टे ज्ञाने ततः परम् ।
विततो व्याप्य विज्ञानं दहत्येव क्षणेन तु ॥३१॥
मनोमयज्ञानमयान्त्सम्यग्दध्वा क्रमेण तु ।
घटस्थदीपवच्छश्वदन्तरेव प्रकाशते ॥३२॥

*ajñānāttu cidābhāso bahistāpena tāpitaḥ*
*dagdham bhavatyeva tadā tūlapiṇḍamivāgninā* (30)
*daharasthaḥ pratyagātmā naṣṭe jñāne tataḥ param*
*vitato vyāpya vijñānaṃ dahatyeva kṣaṇena tu* (31)
*manomayajñānamayāntsamyagdadhvā krameṇa tu*
*ghaṭasthadīpavacchaśvadantareva prakāśate* (32)

**Anvay**

*cidābhāsaḥ*: reflected consciousness; *ajñānāt*: because of its lack of wisdom; *tāpitaḥ*: is burned; *bahiḥ-tāpena*: by an external heat; *tadā iva*: just like; *tūla-piṇḍam*: bale of cotton; *bhavati dagdham*: is burnt; *agninā*: by fire; *jñāne naṣṭe*: when *jñāna* has been destroyed; *pratyagātmā*: inner self; *daharasthaḥ*: located in the ether; *kṣaṇena*: immediately; *param vijñānam*: highest *vijñāna*; *vitataḥ vyāpya*: permeating everything; *dadhvā*: having maintained; *manomaya-jñānamaya-ant*: both *manomaya* and *jñānamaya*; *tu*: now; *dahati*: burns; *krameṇa*: one by one; *tu prakāśate*: then it shines forth; *antar*: from within; *dīp-avacchaśvat*: like a clear light; *ghaṭastha*: inside a pot.

**Translation**

The reflected consciousness, because of its lack of wisdom, is burned by an external heat, just like a bale of cotton is burnt by fire. When *jñāna* has been destroyed, the inner self located in the ether immediately [expresses] the highest *vijñāna*, permeating everything, [and] having maintained both *manomaya* and *jñānamaya*, now burns [them] one by one. Then it shines forth from within, like a clear light inside a pot.

**Commentary**
The ātman, or pure consciousness of the self, abides within beyond the association of the body, mind and senses. Although the essence of existence, it remains unattainable and unknowable, as long as the soul resides in the body. This is the human condition, or we may even say, the human error. As soon as the consciousness is born in the body, it becomes veiled or obscured for the entire duration of one's lifetime. It is not until the time of death, or else by means of certain esoteric practices, that the direct knowledge of the ātman can be regained. The teachings provided in the above verses are meant for this purpose.

The pure consciousness of the ātman remains ever suffused in its own luminosity and bliss. When this consciousness is born in the body, it remains apart, unaffected, and inaccessible in its true state. However, its reflection permeates downward and suffuses the psyche, the mind and senses, and the body with light and life. In this way, human beings are able to function with intelligence and awareness in the different activities and stations of life. As long as this downward reflection of light continues to illumine the person and his life, there will be little memory of or desire to attain the ātman, the sublime consciousness, within. However, for those few individuals, who are nearing completion of their human evolution, the path and practices for attaining the experience of the atman in this lifetime are made available.

The reflected consciousness is considered to be impure at all of its levels due to its association with the mind and body. The ātman is pure knowledge, eternal wisdom, but the reflected consciousness lacks this quality on account of the *vikara*, or impurities, that are stored within it in the form of *saṃskāra*, or worldly impressions. Due to its lack of purity and wisdom, the reflected consciousness is sensitive to and easily affected by the situations, conditions and relations in the world around. It becomes heated and burns on account of adversity, just like a bale of cotton bursts into flame, if burning objects are placed on or near it.

When the mind and senses are withdrawn from the sensory objects, the external knowledge of the world has no access within. Then the ātman, or inner self, which is located in the pure space of consciousness, immediately permeates everything below it with the highest wisdom. Having maintained both the mind and intellect through the reflected light of consciousness, it now burns them both, one by one, with its pure light of wisdom. Free from delusion, the consciousness now shines forth from within, like a clear light inside a pot.

## Verses 33 to 35: Supreme yogi

ध्यायन्नास्ते मुनिश्चैवमासुप्तेरामृतेस्तु यः ।

जीवन्मुक्तः स विज्ञेयः स धन्यः कृतकृत्यवान् ।।३३।।

जीवन्मुक्तपदं त्यक्त्वा स्वदेहे कालसात्कृते ।

विशत्यदेहमुक्तत्वं पवनोऽस्पन्दतमिव ।।३४।।

अशब्दमस्पर्शमरूपमव्ययं तथारसं नित्यमगन्धवच्च यत् ।

अनाद्यनन्तं महतः परं ध्रुवं तदेव शिष्यत्यमलं निरामयम्

।।३५।।

*dhyāyannāste muniścaivamāsupterāmṛtestu yaḥ*
*jīvanmuktaḥ sa vijñeyaḥ sa dhanyaḥ kṛtakṛtyavān* (33)
*jīvanmuktapadaṃ tyaktvā svadehe kālasātkṛte*
*viśatyadehamuktatvaṃ pavano 'spandatamiva* (34)
*aśabdamasparśamarūpamavyayaṃ tathārasaṃ*
*nityamagandhavacca yat*
*anādyanantaṃ mahataḥ paraṃ dhruvaṃ tadeva*
*śiṣyatyamalaṃ nirāmayam* (35)

**Anvay**

*muniḥ*: muni; *yaḥ āste*: who remains; *dhyāyan*: meditating; *evam-āsupteḥ-āmṛteḥ*: right until sleep and death; *vijñeyaḥ jīvanmuktaḥ*: is to be known as a *jīvanmukta*; *kṛtakṛtyavān*: having done his duty; *dhanyaḥ*: blessed; *tyaktvā*: renouncing; *jīvanmukta-padam*: state of jīvanmukta; *svadehe kṛte viśatya*: when his body has decomposed; *kālasāt*: in time; *deha-muktatvam*: liberation from the body; *tam pavanaḥ*: its breath; *aspanda*: unmoving; *tat-eva śiṣyati*: only that remains; *yat*: which; *avyayam*: imperishable; *aśabdam-asparśam-arūpam*: without sound, touch or form; *tathā*: that is; *rasam*: taste; *nityam*: eternal; *ca*: and; *agandhavat*: odourless; *anādi-anantam*: without beginning or end; *mahataḥ param*: beyond the great; *dhruvam*: permanent; *amalam*: pure; *nirāmayam*: untainted.

**Translation**

The muni, who remains meditating right until sleep and death, is to be known as a *jīvanmukta* [who], having done his duty, [is] blessed. Renouncing the state of jīvanmukta, when in time his body has decomposed, [he attains] liberation from the body, its breath unmoving. Only that remains which [is] imperishable, without sound, touch or form, that is, the essence, eternal and odourless, without beginning or end, beyond great, permanent, pure [and] untainted.

**Commentary**

Most people consider themselves in relation to their social status and the work they do, while living in the world. Their life and worth are measured by how active they are, how well they do, and how wealthy they are. But the life of a *muni* is assessed by totally different criteria. The word muni has a more tantric association, as does kundalini yoga, and refers to a yogi, saint, sage or hermit, especially one who remains in silence. At the end of this teaching, we are given the criterion of a muni or yogi, whom we must assume has achieved mastery over the self. The muni is one, who remains in meditation on a daily basis until he sleeps. In this way he passes his life, and remains free from involvement with the world, right up until death.

Such a muni or yogi is known as a *jivanmukta*, liberated, living soul. Having fulfilled the highest duty of man, to attain self-realisation while living, he is truly blessed. At the time of passing, when the breath stops and the body decomposes, he renounces the state of jivanmukta, and attains *dehamukta,* liberation outside the body. When the liberated soul is freed from all vestiges of the physical existence, only the imperishable, pure consciousness remains. Merged in the supreme consciousness, he is beyond the perception of sound, taste, touch, form or smell. He is eternal, untainted, without beginning or end, beyond great.

इत्युपनिषत् ॥

*ityupaniṣat*

Thus [ends] the Upaniṣad.

# Appendices

## 1. Sanskrit text

योगकुण्डल्युपनिषद्योगसिद्धिहृदासनम् ।
निर्विशेषब्रह्मतत्त्वं स्वमात्रमिति चिन्तये ।
ॐ सह नाववत्विति शान्तिः ।।

प्रथमोऽध्याय:

हेतद्वयं हि चित्तस्य वासना च समीरणः ।
तयोर्विनष्ट एकस्मिंस्तदद्वावपि विनश्यतः ।।१।।

तयोरादौ समीरस्य जय कुर्यान्नरः सदा ।
मिताहारश्चासनं च शक्तिचालस्तृतीयकः ।।२।।
एतेषां लक्षनं वक्ष्ये शृणु गौतम सादरम् ।३।

सुस्निग्धमधुराहारश्चतुर्थंशविवर्जितः ।।३।।
भुज्यते शिवसंप्रीत्यै मिताहारः स उच्यते ।४।

आसनं द्विविधं प्रोक्तं पद्मं वज्रासनं तथा ।।४।।
ऊर्वोरुपरि चेद्धत्ते उभे पादतले यथा ।
पद्मासनं भवेदेतत्सर्वपापप्रणाशनम् ।।५।।
वामाङ्घ्रिमूलकन्दाधो ह्यन्यं तदुपरि क्षिपेत् ।
समग्रीवशिरः कायो वज्रासनमितीरितम् ।।६।।

कुण्डल्येव भवेच्छक्तिस्तां तु संचालयेद्बुध ।
स्वस्थानाभा भ्रुवोर्मध्यं शक्तिचालनमुच्यते ।।७।।
तत्साधने द्वयं मुख्यं सरस्वत्सास्तु चालनम् ।

प्राणरोधमथाभ्यासादृज्वी कुण्डलिनी भवेत् ।।८।।
तयोरादौ सरस्वत्याश्चालनं कथयामि ते ।
अरुन्धत्येव कथिता पुराविद्भिः सरस्वती ।।९।।
यस्याः संचालनेनैव स्वयं चलति कुण्डली ।१०।

इडायां वहति प्राणे बद्ध्वा पद्मासनं दृढम् ।।१०।।
द्वादशाङ्गुलदैर्घ्यं च अम्बरं चतुरङ्गुलम् ।
विस्तीर्य तेन तनानाडीं वेष्टयित्वा ततः सुधीः ।।११।।
अङ्गुष्ठतर्जनीभ्यां तु हस्ताभ्यां धारयेद्द्वढम् ।
स्वशक्त्या चालयेद्वामे दक्षिणेन पुनःपुनः ।।१२।।
मुहूर्तद्वयपर्यन्तं निर्भयाच्चालयेत्सुधीः ।
ऊर्ध्वमाकर्षयेत्किंचित्सुषुम्नां कुण्डलीगताम् ।।१३।।
तेन कुण्डलिनी तस्याः सुषुम्नाया मुखं व्रजेत् ।
जहाति तस्मात्प्राणोऽयं सुषुम्नां व्रजति स्वतः ।।१४।।
तुन्दे तु तानं कुर्याच्च कण्ठसंकोचने कृते ।
सरस्वत्यां चालनेन वक्षसश्चोर्ध्वगो मरुत् ।।१५।।
सूर्येण रेचयेद्वायुं सरस्वत्यास्तु चालने ।
कण्ठसंकोचनं कृत्वा वक्षसश्चोर्ध्वगो मरुत् ।।१६।।
तस्मात्संचालयेन्नित्यं शब्दगर्भा सरस्वतीम् ।
यस्याः संचालनेनैव योगी रोगैः प्रमुच्यते ।।१७।।
गुल्मं जलोदरः प्लीहा ये चान्ये तुन्दमध्यगाः ।
सर्वे ते शक्तिचालेन रोगा नायन्ति निश्चयम् ।।१८।।

प्राणरोधमथेदानीं प्रवक्ष्यामि समासतः ।
प्राणश्च देहयो वायुरायामः कुम्भकः स्मृतिः ।।१९।।

स एव द्विविधः प्रोक्तः सहितः केवलस्तथा ।
यावत्केवलसिद्धिः स्यात्तावत्सहितमभ्यसेत् ।।२०।।
सूर्योज्जायी शीतली च भस्त्री चैव चतुर्थिका ।
भेदैरेव समं कुम्भो यः स्यात्सहितकुम्भकः ।।२१।।

पवित्रे निर्जने देशे शर्करादिविवर्जिते ।
धनुःप्रमाणपर्यन्ते शीताग्निजलवर्जिते ।।२२।।
पवित्रे नात्युच्चनीचे ह्यासने सुखदे सखे ।
बद्धपद्मासनं कृत्वा सरस्वत्यास्तु चालनम् ।।२३।।

दक्षनाड्या समाकृष्य बहिष्ठं पवनं शनैः ।
यथेष्टं पूरयेद्वायुं रेचयेदिडया ततः ।।२४।।
कपालशोधने वापि रेचयेत्पवनं शनैः ।
चतुष्कं वातदोषं तु कृमिदोषं निहन्ति च ।।२५।।
पुनः पुनरिदं कार्यं सूर्यभेददमुदाहृतम् ।२६।

मुखं संयम्यं नाडिभ्यामाकृष्य पवनं शनैः ।।२६।।
यथा लगति कण्ठात्तु हृदयावधि सस्वनम् ।
पूर्ववत्कुम्भयेत्प्राणं रेचयेदिडया ततः ।।२७।।
शीर्षोदितानलहरं गलश्लेष्महरं परम् ।
सर्वरोगहरं पुण्यं देहानलविवर्धनम् ।।२८।।
नाडीजलोदरं धातुगतदोषविनाशनम् ।
गच्छतस्तिष्ठतः कार्यमुज्जायाख्यं तु कुम्भकम् ।।२९।।

जिह्वया वायुमाकृष्य पूर्ववत्कुम्भकादनु ।
शनैस्तु घ्राणरन्ध्राभ्यां रेचयेदनिलं सुधीः ।।३०।।

गुल्मप्लीहादिकान्दोषान्क्षयं पित्तं ज्वरं तृषाम् ।
विषाणि शीतली नाम कुम्भकोऽयं निहन्ति च ।।३१।।

ततः पद्मासनं बद्ध्वा समग्रीवोदरः सुधीः ।
मुखं संयम्य यत्नेन प्राणं घ्राणेन रेचयेत् ।।३२।।
यथा लगति कण्ठात्तु कपाले सस्वनं ततः ।
वेगेन पूरयेत् किंचिद्धृत्पद्मावधि मारुतम् ।।३३।।
पुनर्विरेचयेत्तद्वत्पूरयेच्च पुनः पुनः ।
यथैव लोहकाराणां भस्त्रा वेगेन चाल्यते ।।३४।।
यथैव स्वशरीरस्थं चालयेत्पवनं शनैः ।
यथा श्रमो भवेद्देह तथा सूर्येण पूरयेत् ।।३५।।
यथोदरं भवेत्पूर्णं पवनेन तथा लघु ।
धारयन्नासिकामध्यं तर्जनीभ्यां विना दृढम् ।।३६।।
कुम्भकं पूर्ववत्कृत्वा रेचयेदिडयानिलम् ।
कण्ठोत्थितानलहरं शरीराग्निविवर्दनम् ।।३७।।
कुण्डलीबोदहकं पुण्यं पापघ्नं शुभदं सुखम् ।
ब्रह्मनाडीमुखान्तस्थकफाद्दर्गलनाशनम् ।।३८।।
गुणत्रयसमुद्भूतग्रन्थित्रयविभेदकम् ।
विशेषेणैव कर्तव्यं भस्त्राख्यं कुम्भकं त्विदम् ।।३९।।

चतुर्णामपि भेदानां कुम्भके समुपस्थिते ।
बन्धत्रयमिदं कार्यं योगिभिर्वीतकल्मशैः ।।४०।।
प्रथमो मूलबन्धस्तु द्वितीयोड्डीयणाभिधः ।
जालन्धरस्तृतीयस्तु तेषां लक्षणमुच्यते ।।४१।।

अधोगतिमपानं वै ऊर्ध्वगं कुरुते बलात् ।

आकुञ्चनेन तं प्रहुर्मूलबन्धोऽयमुच्यते ।।४२।।
अपाने चोर्ध्वगे याते संप्राप्ते वह्निमण्डले ।
ततो ऽनलशिखा दीर्घा वर्धते वायुनाहता ।।४३।।
ततो यातौ वह्न्यपानौ प्राणमुष्णस्वरूपकम् ।
तेनात्यन्तप्रदीप्तेन ज्वलनो देहजस्तथा ।।४४।।
तेन कुण्डलिनी सुप्ता संतप्ता संप्रबुध्यते ।
दण्डाहतभुजङ्गेव निःश्वस्य ऋजुतां व्रजेत् ।।४५।।
बिलप्रवेशितो यत्र ब्रह्मनाड्यन्तरं व्रजेत् ।
तस्मान्नित्यं मूलबन्धः कर्तव्यो योगिभिः सदा ।।४६।।

कुम्भकान्ते रेचकादौ कर्तव्यस्तूड्डियाणकः ।
बन्धो येन सुषुम्नायां प्राणस्तूड्डीयते यतः ।।४७।।
तस्मादुड्डीयणाख्योऽयं योगिभिः समुदाहृतः ।
सति वज्रासने पादौ कराभ्या धारयेद्दृढम् ।।४८।।
गुल्फदेशसमीपे च कन्दं तत्र प्रपीडेत् ।
पश्चिमं ताणमुदरे धारयेद्धृदये गले ।।४९।।
शनैः शनैर्यदा प्राणस्तुन्दसन्धिं निगच्छति ।
तुन्ददोषं विनिर्धूय कर्तव्यं सततं शनैः ।।५०।।

पूरकान्ते तु कर्तव्यो बन्धो जालन्धराभिधः ।
कण्ठसंकोचरूपोऽसौ वायुमार्गनिरोधकः ।।५१।।
अधस्तात्कुञ्चनेनाशु कण्ठसंकोचने कृते ।
मध्ये पश्चिमताणेन स्यात्प्राणो ब्रह्मनाडिगः ।।५२।।
पूर्वोक्तेन क्रमेणैव सम्यगासनमास्थितः
चालनं तु सरस्वत्याः कृत्वा प्राणं निरोधयेत् ।।५३।।

प्रथमे दिवसे कार्यं कुम्भकानां चुतष्यम् ।
प्रत्येकं दशसंख्याकं द्वितीये पञ्चभिस्तथा ।।५४।।
विंशत्यलं तृतीयेऽह्नि पञ्चवृद्ध्या दिनेदिने ।
कर्तव्यः कुम्भको नित्यं बन्धत्रयसमन्वितः ।।५५।।

दिवा सुप्तिर्निशायां तु जागरादतिमैथुनात् ।
बहुसंक्रमणं नित्यं रोधान्मूत्रपुरीषयोः ।।५६।।
विषमाशनदोषाच्च प्रयासप्राणचिन्तनात् ।
शीघ्रमुत्पद्यते रोगः स्तम्भयेद्यदि संयमी ।।५७।।
योगाभ्यासेन मे रोग उत्पन्न इति कथ्यते ।
ततोऽभ्यासं त्यजेदेवं प्रथमं विघ्नोच्यते ।।५८।।

द्वितीय संशयाख्यं च तृतीयं च प्रमत्तता ।
आलस्याख्यं चतुर्थं च निद्रारूपं तु पञ्चमम् ।।५९।।
षष्ठं तु विरतिर्भ्रान्तिः सप्तमं परिकीर्तितम् ।
विषमं चाष्टमं चैव अनास्था नवमं स्मृतम् ।।६०।।
अलब्धिर्योगतत्त्वस्य दशमं प्रोच्यते बुधैः ।
इत्येतद्विघ्नदशकं विचारेण त्यजेद्बुधः ।।६१।।

प्राणाभ्यासस्ततः कार्यो नित्यं सत्त्वस्थया धिया ।
सुषुम्ना लीयते चित्तं तथा वायुः प्रधावति ।।६२।।
शुष्के मले तु योगी च स्याद्गतिश्चलिता ततः ।
अधोगतिमपानं वै उर्ध्वगं कुरुते बलात् ।।६३।।
आकुञ्चनेन तं प्राहुर्मूलबन्धोऽयमुच्यते ।
अपानश्चोर्ध्वगो भूत्वा वह्निना सह गच्छति ।।६४।।
प्राणस्थानं ततो वह्निः प्राणापानौ च सत्वरम् ।

मिलित्वा कुण्डलीं याति प्रसुप्ता कुण्डलाकृतिः ।।६५।।

तेनाग्निना च संतप्ता पवनेनैव चालिता ।
प्रसार्यं स्वशरीरं तु सुषुम्ना वदनान्तरें ।।६६।।
ब्रह्मग्रन्थिं ततो भित्त्वा रजोगुणसमुद्भवम् ।
सुषुम्ना वदने शीघ्रं विद्युल्लेखेव संस्फुरेत् ।।६७।।
विष्णुग्रन्थिं प्रयात्युच्चैः सत्वरं हृदि संस्थिता ।
ऊर्ध्वं गच्छति यच्चास्ते रुद्रग्रन्थिं तदुद्भवम् ।।६८।।
भ्रुवोर्मध्यं तु संभिद्य याति शीतांशुमण्डलम् ।६९।

अनाहताख्यं यच्चक्रं दलैः षोडशभिर्युतम् ।।६९।।
तत्र शीतांशुसंजातं द्रवं शोषयति स्वयम्
चलिते प्राणवेगेन रक्तं पित्तं रवेर्ग्रहात् ।।७०।।
यातेन्दुचक्रं यत्रास्ते शुद्धश्लेष्मद्रवात्मकम् ।
तत्र सिक्तं ग्रसत्युष्णं कथं शीतस्वभावकम् ।।७१।।
तथैव रभसा शुक्लं चन्द्ररूपं हि तप्यते ।
ऊर्ध्वं प्रवर्ति क्षुब्धा तदैवं भ्रमतेतराम् ।।७२।।
तस्यास्वादवशाच्चित्तं बहिष्ठं विषयेषु यत् ।
तदेव परं भुक्त्वा स्वस्थः स्वात्मरतो युवा ।।७३।।

प्रकृत्यष्टकरूपं च स्थानं गच्छति कुण्डली ।
क्रोडीकृत्य शिवं याति क्रोडीकृत्य विलीयते ।।७४।।
इत्यधोर्ध्वरजः शुक्लं शिवे तदनु मारुतः ।
प्राणापानौ समा याति सदा जातौ तथैव च ।।७५।।
भूतेऽल्पे चाप्यनल्पे वा वाचके त्वतिवर्धते ।
धावयत्यखिला वाता अग्निमूषाहिरण्यवत् ।।७६।।

आधिभौतिकदेहं तु आधिदैविकविग्रहे ।
देहोऽतिविमलं याति जातिवाहिकतामियात् ।।७७।।
जाड्यभावविनिर्मुक्तममलं चिन्मयात्मकम् ।
तस्यातिवाहिकं मुख्यं सर्वेषां तु मदात्मकम् ।।७८।।

जायाभवविनिर्मुक्तः कालरूपस्य विभ्रमः ।
इति तं स्वस्वरूपा हि मति रज्जुभुजङ्गवत् ।।७९।।
मृषैवोदेति सकलं मृषैव प्रविलीयते ।
रौप्यबुद्धिः शुक्तिकायां स्त्रीपुंसोर्भ्रमतो यथा ।।८०।।
पिण्डब्रह्माण्डयोरैक्यं लिङ्गसूत्रात्मनोरपि ।
स्वापाव्याकृतयोरैक्यं स्वप्रकाशचिदात्मनोः ।।८१।।

शक्तिः कुण्डलिनी नाम बिसतन्तुनिभा शुभा ।
मूलकन्दं फणाग्रेण दृष्ट्वा कमलकन्दवत् ।।८२।।
मुखेन पुच्छं संगृह्य ब्रह्मरन्ध्रसमन्विता ।८३।

पद्मासनगतः स्वस्थो गुदमाकुञ्च्य साधकः ।।८३।।
वायुमूर्ध्वगतं कुर्वन्कुम्भकाविष्टमानसः ।
वाय्वाघातवशादग्निः स्वाधिष्ठानगतो ज्वलन् ।।८४।।
ज्वलनाघातपवना घातोरुन्निद्रितोऽहिरात् ।
ब्रह्मग्रन्थिं ततो भित्त्वा विष्णुग्रन्थिं भिनत्त्यतः ।।८५।।
रुद्रग्रन्थिं च भित्त्वैव कमलानि भिनत्ति षट् ।
सहस्राकमले शक्तिः शिवेन सह मोदते ।।८६।।
सैववस्था परा ज्ञेया सैव निर्वृतिकारिणी इति ।।८७।।

द्वितीयोऽध्याय:

अथाहं संप्रवक्ष्यामि विद्यां खेचरीसंज्ञिकाम् ।
यथा विज्ञानवानस्या लोकेऽस्मिन्नजरोऽमरः ।।१।।
मृत्युव्याधिजराग्रस्तो दृष्ट्वा विद्यामिमां मुने ।
बुद्धिं दृढतरां कृत्वा खेचरीं तु समभ्यसेत् ।।२।।
जरामृत्युगदघ्नो यः खेचरीं वेत्ति भूतले ।
ग्रन्थतश्चर्थतश्चैव तदभ्यासप्रयोगतः ।।३।।
तं मुने सर्वभावेन गुरुं मत्या समाश्रयेत् ।४।

दुर्लभा खेचरी विद्या तदभ्यासोऽपि दुर्लभः ।।४।।
अभ्यासं मेलनं चैव युगपन्नैव सिध्यति ।
अभ्यासमात्रनिरता न विन्दन्ते ह मेलनम् ।।५।।
अभ्यासं लभते ब्रह्मञ्जन्मान्तरे क्वचित् ।
मेलनं तत्तु जन्मनां शतान्तेऽपि न लभ्यते ।।६।।
अभ्यासं बहुजन्मान्ते कृत्वा तद्भावसाधितम् ।
मेलनं लभते कश्चिद्योगी जन्मान्तरे क्वचित् ।।७।।
यदा तु मेलनं योगी लभते गुरुवक्त्रतः ।
तदा तत्सिद्धिमाप्नोति यदुक्ता शास्त्रसंततौ ।।८।।
ग्रन्थतश्चार्थतश्चैव मेलनं लभते यदा ।
तदा शिवात्वमाप्नोति निर्मुक्तः सर्वसंसृतेः ।।९।।
शास्त्रं विनापि संबोद्धुं गुरवोऽपि न शक्नुयुः ।
तस्मात्सुदुर्लभतरं लभ्यं शास्त्रमिदं मुने ।।१०।।

यावन्न लभ्यते शास्त्रं तावद्गां पर्यटेद्यतिः ।
यदा संलभ्यते शास्त्रं तदा सिद्धिः करे स्थिता ।।११।।
न शास्त्रेण विना सिद्धिर्दृष्टा चैव जगत्त्रये ।

तस्मान्मेलनदातारं शास्त्रदातारमच्युतम् ।।१२।।
तदभ्यासप्रदातारं शिवं मत्वा समाश्रयेत् ।
लब्ध्वा शास्त्रमिदं मह्यमन्येषां न प्रकाशयेत् ।।१३।।
तस्मात्सर्वप्रयत्नेन गोपनैयं विजञानता ।
यत्रास्ते च गुरुर्ब्रह्मन्दिव्ययोगप्रदायकः ।।१४।।
तत्र गत्वा च तेनोक्तविद्यां संगृह्य खेचरीम् ।
तेनोक्तः संयगभ्यासं कुर्यादावतन्द्रितः ।।१५।।
अनया विद्यया योगी खेचरीसिद्धिभाग्भवेत् ।१६।

खेचर्या खेचरीं युञ्जन्खेचरीबीजपूरया ।।१६।।
खेचराधिपतिर्भूत्वा खेचरेषु सदा वसेत् ।
खेचरावसथं वह्निमम्बुमण्डल भूषितम् ।।१७।।
आख्यातं खेचरीबीजं तेन योगः प्रसिध्यति ।१८।

सोमांशनवकं वर्णं प्रतिलोमेन चोद्धरेत् ।।१८।।
तस्मात्त्र्यंशकमाख्यातमक्षरं चन्द्ररूपकम् ।
तस्मादप्यष्टमं वर्णं विलोमेन परं मुने ।।१९।।
तथा तत्परमं विद्धि तदादिरपि पञ्चमी ।
इन्दोश्च बहुभिन्ने च कूटोऽयं परिकीर्तितः ।।२०।।
गुरूपदेशलभ्यं च सर्वयोगप्रसिद्धीदम् ।२१।

यत्तस्य देहजा माया निरुद्धकरणाश्रया ।।२१।।
स्वप्नेऽपि न लभेत्तस्य नित्यं द्वादशजप्यतः ।
य इमां पञ्च लक्षाणि जपेदपि सुयन्त्रितः ।।२२।।
तस्य श्रीखेचरीसिद्धिः स्वयमेव प्रवर्तते ।
नश्यन्ति सर्वविघ्नानि प्रसीदन्ति च देवताः ।।२३।।

वलीपलितनाशश्च भविष्यति न संशयः ।२४।

एवं लब्ध्वा महाविद्यामभ्यासं कारयेत्ततः ।।२४।।
अन्यथा क्लिश्यते ब्रह्मन्न सिद्धिः खेचरीपथे ।
यदभ्यासविधौ विद्यां न लभेद्यः सुधामयीम् ।।२५।।
ततः संमेलकादौ च लब्ध्वा विद्यां सदा जपेत् ।
नान्यथा रहितो ब्रह्मन्न किंचित्सिद्धिभाग्भवेत् ।।२६।।
यदीदं लभ्यते शास्त्रं तदा विद्यां समाश्रयेत् ।
ततस्तदोदितां सिद्धिमाशु तां लभते मुनिः ।।२७।।

तालुमूलं समुत्कृष्य सप्तवासरमात्मवित् ।
स्वगुरूक्तप्रकारेण मलं सर्वं विशोधयेत् ।।२८।।
स्नुहिपत्रनिभं शस्त्रं सुतीक्ष्णं स्निग्धनिर्मलम् ।
समादाय ततस्तेन रोममात्रं समुच्छिनेत् ।।२९।।
हित्वा सैन्धवपथ्याभ्यां चूर्णिताभ्यां प्रकर्षयेत् ।
पुनः सप्तदिने प्राप्ते रोममात्रं समुच्छिनेत् ।।३०।।
एवं क्रमेण षन्मासं नित्योद्युक्तः समाचरेत् ।
षण्मासाद्रसनामूलं शिराबद्धं प्रणश्यति ।।३१।।
अथ वागीश्वरीधाम शिरो वस्त्रेण वेष्टयेत् ।
शनैरुत्कर्षयेद्योगी कालवेलाविधानवित् ।।३२।।
पुनः षण्मासमात्रेण नित्यं संघर्षणान्मुने ।
भ्रूमध्यावधि चाप्येति तिर्यक्कर्णबिलावधिः ।।३३।।
अधश्च चुबुकं मूलं प्रयाति क्रमचारिता ।
पुनः संवत्सराणां तु तृतीयादेव लीलया ।।३४।।
केशान्तमूर्ध्वं क्रामति तिर्यक्शाखावधिर्मुने ।

अधस्तात्कण्ठकूपान्तं पुनर्वर्षत्रयेण तु ।।३५।।
ब्रह्मरन्ध्रं समावृत्य तिष्ठेदेव न संशयः ।
तिर्यक् चूलितलं याति अधः कण्ठबिलावधि ।।३६।।
शनैः शनैर्मस्तकाच्च महावज्रकपाटभित् ।३७।

पूर्वं बीजयुता विद्या ह्याख्याता यातिदुर्लभा ।।३७।।
तस्याः षडङ्गं कुर्वीतं तया षट्स्वरभिन्नया ।
कुर्यादेवं करन्यासं सर्वसिद्ध्यादिहेतवे ।।३८।।
शनैरेवं प्रकर्तव्यमभ्यासं युगपन्नहि ।
युगपद्वर्तते यस्य शरीरं विलयं व्रजेत् ।।३९।।
तस्माच्छनैः शनैः कार्यमभ्यासं मुनिपुङ्गव ।४०।

तदा च बाह्यमार्गेण जिह्वा ब्रह्मबिलं व्रजेत् ।।४०।।
तदा ब्रह्मार्गलं ब्रह्मन्दुर्भेद्यं त्रिदशनैरपि ।
अङ्गुल्यग्रेण संघृष्य जिह्वामात्रं निवेशयेत् ।।४१।।
एवं वर्षत्रयं कृत्वा ब्रह्मद्वारं प्रविश्यति ।
ब्रह्मद्वारे प्रविष्टे तु सम्यङ्मथनमाचरेत् ।।४२।।
मथनेन विना किञ्चित्साधयन्ति विपश्चिताः ।
खेचरीमन्त्रसिद्धस्य सिध्यां मथनेन विना ।।४३।।
जपं च मथनं चैव कृत्वा शीघ्रं फलं लभेत् ।४४।

स्वर्णजां रौप्यजां वापि लोहजां वा शलाकिकाम् ।।४४।।
नियोच्य नासिकारन्ध्रं दुग्ध सिक्तेन तन्तुना ।
प्राणान्निरुध्य हृदये सुखमासनमात्मनः ।।४५।।
शनैः सुमथनं कुर्याद्भ्रूमध्ये न्यस्य चक्षुषी ।
षण्मासं मथनावस्था भावेनैव प्रजायते ।।४६।।

यथा सुषुप्तिर्बालानां यथा भवस्तथा भरेत् ।
न सदा मथनं शस्तं मासे समाचरेत् ।।४७।।
सदा रसनया योगी मार्गं न परिसंक्रमेत् ।
एवं द्वादशवर्षान्ते संसिद्धिर्भवति ध्रुवा ।।४८।।
शरिरे सकलं विश्वं पश्यन्त्यात्माविभेदतः ।
ब्रह्माण्डोऽयं महामार्गो राजदन्तोर्ध्वकुण्डली ।।४९।। इति ।।

तृतियोऽध्यायः

मेलनमनुः । ह्रीं भं सं पं फं सं क्षं ।
पद्मज उवाच ।

अमावास्या च प्रतिपत्पौर्णमासी च शंकर ।
अस्याः का वर्ण्यते संज्ञा एतदाख्याहि तत्त्वतः ।।१।।
प्रतिपद्दिनती 'काले अमावास्या तथैव च ।
पौर्णमास्यां स्थिरीकुर्यात्स च पन्था हि नान्यथा ।।२।।

कामेन विषयाकाङ्क्षी विषयात्काममोहितः ।
द्वावेव संत्यजेन्नित्यं निरञ्जनमुपाश्रयेत् ।।३।।
अपरं संत्यजेत्सर्वं यदिच्छेदात्मनो हितम् ।४।

शक्तिमध्ये मनः कृत्वा मनः शक्तेश्च मध्यगम् ।।४।।
मनसा मन आलोक्य तत्त्यजेत्परं पदम् ।
मन एव हि बिन्दुश्च उत्पत्तिस्थितिकारणम् ।।५।।
मनसोत्पद्यते बिन्दुर्यथा क्षीरं घृतात्मकम् ।
न च बन्धनमध्यस्थं तद्वे कारणमानसम् ।।६।।
चन्द्रार्कमध्यमा शक्तिर्यत्रस्था तत्र बन्धनम् ।७।

ज्ञात्वा सुषुम्नां तद्भेदं कृत्वा वायुं च मध्यगम् ।।७।।
स्थित्वासौवैन्दवस्थाने घ्राणरन्ध्रे निरोधयेत् ।
वायुं बिन्दुं समाख्यातं सत्त्वं प्रकृतिमेव च ।।८।।
षट् चक्राणि परिज्ञत्वा प्रविशेत्सुखमण्डलम् ।९।

मूलाधार स्वाधिष्ठानं मणिपुरं तृतीयकम् ।।९।।
अनाहतं विशुद्धं च आज्ञाचक्रं च षष्ठकम् ।
आधारं गुदमित्युक्तं स्वाधिष्ठानं तु लैङ्गिकम् ।।१०।।
मणिपुरं नाभिदेशं हृदयस्थमनाहतम् ।
विशुद्धिः कण्ठमूले च आज्ञाचक्रं च मस्तकम् ।।११।।
षट् चक्राणि परिज्ञत्वा प्रविशेत्सुखमण्डले ।
प्रविशेद्वायुमाकृष्य तयैवोर्ध्वं नियोजयेत् ।।१२।।
एवं समभ्यसेद्वायुं स ब्रह्माण्डमयो भवेत् ।
वायुं बिन्दुं तथा चक्रं चित्तं चैव समभ्यसेत् ।।१३।।

समाधिमेकेन समममृतं यान्ति योगिनः ।
यथाग्निर्दारुमध्यस्थो नोत्तिष्ठेन्मथनं विना ।।१४।।
विना चाभ्यासयोगेन जज्ञानदीपस्तथा न हि ।
घटमध्यगतो दीपो बाह्ये नैव प्रकाशते ।।१५।।
भिन्ने तस्मिन्घटे चैव दीपज्वाला च भासते ।
स्वकायं घटमित्युक्तं यथा दीपो हि तत्पदम् ।।१६।।
गुरुवाक्यसमाभिन्ने ब्रह्मज्ञानं स्फुटीभवेत् ।
कर्णधारं गुरुं प्राप्य कृत्वा सूक्षमं तरन्ति च ।।१७।।
अभ्यासवासनाशक्त्या तरन्ति भवसागरम् ।१८।

परायामङ्कुरीभूया पश्यन्त्यां द्विदलीकृता ।।१८।।

मध्यमायां मुकुलिता वैखर्यां विकसीकृता ।
पूर्वं यथोदिता या वाग्विलोमेनास्तगा भवेत् ।।१९।।
तस्या वाचः परो देवः कूटस्थो वाक्प्रबोधकः ।
सोहमस्मीति निश्चित्य यः सदा वर्तते पुमान् ।।२०।।
शब्दैरुच्चावचैर्नीचैर्भाषितोऽपि न लिप्यते ।२१।

विश्वश्च तैजसश्चैव प्राज्ञश्चेति च ते त्रयः ।।२१।।
विराड्ढिरण्यगर्भश्च ईश्वरश्चेति ते त्रयः ।
ब्रह्माण्डं चैव पिण्डाण्दं लोका भूरादयः क्रमात् ।।२२।।
स्वस्वोपाधिलयादेव लीयन्ते प्रत्यगात्मनि ।
अण्डं ज्ञानाग्निना तप्तं लीयते कारणैः सह ।।२३।।
परमात्मनि लीनं तत्परं ब्रह्मैव जायते ।
ततः स्तिमितगम्भीरं तेजो न  तमस्ततम् ।।२४।।
अनाख्यमनभिव्यक्तं सत्किंचिदवशिष्यते ।
ध्यात्वा मध्यस्थमात्मानं कलसान्तरदीपवत् ।।२५।।
अङ्गुष्ठमात्रमात्मानमधूमज्योतिरूपकम् ।
प्रकाशयन्तमन्तस्स्थं ध्यायेत्कूटस्थमव्ययम् ।।२६।।

विज्ञानात्मा तथा देहे जाग्रत्स्वप्नसुषुप्तितः ।
मायया मोहितः पश्चाद्बहुजन्मान्तरे पुनः ।।२७।।
सत्कर्मपरिपाकात्तु स्वविकारं चिकीर्षति ।
कोऽहं कथमयं दोषः संसाराख्य उपागतः ।।२८।।
जाग्रत्स्वप्ने व्यवहरन्त्सुषुप्तौ क्व गतिर्मम ।
इति चिन्तापरो भूत्वा स्वभासा च विशेषतः ।।२९।।

अज्ञानात्तु चिदाभासो बहिस्तापेन तापितः ।

दग्धं भवत्येव तदा तूलपिण्डमिवाग्निना ॥३०॥
दहरस्थः प्रत्यगात्मा नष्टे ज्ञाने ततः परम् ।
विततो व्याप्य विज्ञानं दहत्येव क्षणेन तु ॥३१॥
मनोमयज्ञानमयान्त्सम्यग्दध्वा क्रमेण तु ।
घटस्थदीपवच्छश्वदन्तरेव प्रकाशते ॥३२॥

ध्यायन्नास्ते मुनिश्चैवमासुप्तेरामृतेस्तु यः ।
जीवन्मुक्तः स विज्ञेयः स धन्यः कृतकृत्यवान् ॥३३॥
जीवन्मुक्तपदं त्यक्त्वा स्वदेहे कालसात्कृते ।
विशत्यदेहमुक्तत्वं पवनोऽस्पन्दतमिव ॥३४॥
अशब्दमस्पर्शमरूपमव्ययं तथारसं नित्यमगन्धवच्च यत् ।
अनाद्यनन्तं महतः परं ध्रुवं तदेव शिष्यत्यमलं निरामयम्
॥३५॥

इत्युपनिषत् ॥

## 2. Pronunciation Guide

| | |
|---|---|
| a | nut |
| ā | father |
| i | bit |
| ī | knee |
| u | hook |
| ū | sue |
| ṛ | hurt |
| e | net |
| ai | time |
| o | got |
| au | house |
| ṃ | hum |
| ḥ | h + preceding vowel |
| k | paprika |
| kh | ink horn |
| g | ago |
| gh | big hut |
| ṅ | anger |
| c | chat |
| ch | much harm |
| j | jog |
| jh | raj house |
| ñ | engine |
| ṭ | borscht |
| ṭh | borscht home |
| ḍ | fresh dill |
| ḍh | flushed heart |
| ṇ | rainy |
| t | tarp |
| th | scout hall |
| d | modern |
| dh | mud hut |
| n | banal |
| p | papa |

| | |
|---|---|
| ph | top half |
| b | maybe |
| bh | mob hall |
| m | chroma |
| y | young |
| r | merit |
| l | alas |
| v | lava |
| ś | shin |
| ṣ | sunshine |
| h | hut |

## 3. Continuous Translation

**Invocation**

Thus I meditated on the seat of the heart, [which is] the power of yoga, on the upanishad of yoga kuṇḍalī, being nothing but the undiscriminating, true knowledge of Brahma. Saying: Om, may this teaching benefit both of us together. Peace.

**Chapter One**

1.

The two causes of individual consciousness [are] the mental disposition and vital energy. If one of these two is destroyed, then both are destroyed.

2, 3a.

Of these two, a man should always control the prāṇa first (by) moderation in diet, (second) posture and thirdly, rotation and control of the pranic force. I shall describe the characteristics of these. Listen attentively, Gautama.

3b, 4a.

A soft, sweet offering should be consumed, without filling one fourth [of the stomach] in order to please Śiva. This is called moderation in diet.

4b-6.

Then posture is declared [to be] of two kinds: *padma* [and] *vajra*. It is *padmāsana* if both soles of the feet are placed on top of the thighs; this destroys all sins. It is said [to be] *vajrāsana* [when] one places the opposite foot below the *mūlakanda*, the other above it, the neck, head [and] body upright.

7-10a.

Śakti is really kuṇḍalinī. A wise person should move it up [from] its location [to] the navel [and] to the eyebrow centre. [This] is called *śakticāla*. To achieve this, two [things] are essential: *sarasvatīcāla* [and] control of prāṇa. Then, through practice, the kuṇḍalinī becomes straight. Of these two, I shall describe to you first sarasvatīcāla. It is told by those who know the past [that] Sarasvatī [is] really Arundhatī. Only by arousing her will kuṇḍalinī arise spontaneously.

10b-18.

When the prāṇa passes through *iḍā*, [then] the wise man, firmly bound [in] padmāsana, having expanded the nāḍī the length [of] twelve fingers and circumference [of] four fingers, should hold [the lower ribs] continually enclosing [them] with the thumb [and] forefingers of both hands, [and] repeatedly stir up the śakti from right to left. The wise man should stir [it] up fearlessly for the duration [of] two muhūrtas. He should draw [it] upwards a little [so that] the kuṇḍalinī goes into *suṣumnā.*

Thus kuṇḍalinī enters the mouth of the suṣumnā. The prāṇa departs from there [and] enters suṣumnā of its own accord. He should expand the abdomen by contracting the throat. By agitating in *sarasvatī*, the prāṇa, going upwards, [reaches] the chest. He should exhale through the right nostril, [while] continuing to agitate *sarasvatī* [and] contracting the throat, the prāṇa goes upwards [from] the chest. Therefore he should continually stir up sarasvatī [whose] womb [is of] sound. Simply by arousing her, the yogin is freed from disease. Diseases of the spleen, dropsy, and all other diseases arising within the abdomen are certainly prevented by *śakticāla.*

19-21.

So now, I shall explain succinctly the suppression of prāṇa. Prāṇa is the movement [of] vital air in the body and [its retention] is called *kumbhaka.* It is said [to be] just of two kinds, *sahita* and *kevala.* As long as he practises *sahita*, he will have the power of *kevala*. The closing of the nostrils and the mouth [is] the same in the four parts, namely *sūrya, ujjāyī, śītalī* and *bhastrī.* This is *sahita kumbhaka*.

22-23.
Seated firmly in *padmāsana* on a pleasant [and] favourable seat [which is] pure [and] not too high or low, in a sacred [and] solitary place free from grit etc, of the length [of] a bow, without cold, fire [or] water, he should remain stirring up sarasvatī.

24-26a.
Having slowly drawn in the air from outside through the right nostril, he should inhale for as long as he wants, [and] then exhale through the left [nostril]. After purifying the skull, he should exhale slowly. [This] destroys the four *vāta* diseases and the disease of worms. This should be done repeatedly. This is called *sūryabheda.*

26b-29.
Slowly drawing in the breath through both nostrils, mouth closed, he holds its sound from the throat to the heart as long as [he wishes]. He restrains the prāṇa as before, then exhales through the left [nostril]. [This] destroys the fire produced [in] the head, the phlegm [in] the throat [and] afterwards destroys all sicknesses, [thereby] increasing the digestive power [in] the body [and] purifying [it]. It removes diseases arising in the nāḍīs, *jalodara* [and] *dhātus.* This kumbhaka is called ujjāyī [and] is to be done walking or standing.

30-31.
After drawing in the breath through the tongue, then retaining [it] as before, the wise man should slowly exhale through both nostrils. This breath retention called *śītalī* causes the removal [of] diseases such as *gulma*, *plīha*, bile, fever, thirst and poisons.

32-39.
Then, the wise man having assumed padmāsana, neck and abdomen upright, mouth closed, should exhale with effort through the nose. As soon as this ensues, he should draw the breath with force upwards from the feet, then loudly from the

neck into the skull, holding [it] a while. In the same way he should exhale again, and inhale again and again. Just as the bellows of blacksmiths are moved with force, so he should slowly move the air within his own body. If the body becomes weary, then he should inhale through the right nostril. If the belly becomes full of air, then quickly pressing the centre [of] the nostrils firmly [but] not with the forefingers, [and] retaining the breath as before, he should exhale through the left nostril.

40-41.
Through those four means, when kumbhaka is imminent, these three bandhas should be performed by the yogins, who are untainted. The first [is] *mūlabandha*; the second is called *uḍḍīyana* and the third *jālandhara.* A detailed description of them is given [here].

42-46.
*Apāna,* [which has] a downward movement, is forcibly made [to] go upwards by bending forward. This offering is called *mūlabandha*. And when *apāna* goes upwards, arriving at the sphere [of] agni, then the flame [of] agni grows long, buffeted by *vāyu*. Then agni and apāna, in the form [of] heat, enter prāṇa. Through this [process], a powerfully blazing fire is thus produced in the body, [and] so the sleeping kuṇḍalinī is awakened [by] its glowing heat. [Then the kuṇḍalinī], hissing, becomes erect like a snake struck [by] a stick. It enters the opening [of] *brahmanāḍi,* moving inside there. Therefore, mūlabandha should always be practised daily by the yogins.

47-50.
Now *uḍḍīyaṇa* should be performed at the end of kumbhaka [and] the beginning of exhalation. Because through this [practice] prāṇa flies up suṣumnā, this bandha is therefore called *uḍḍīyaṇa* by yogins. Remaining in *vajrāsana*, one should firmly grasp the feet with both hands, and press there the *kanda* [at] the place near the ankles. One should very

slowly hold the [awareness] at the back side [of] the thread or nāḍī in the abdomen, heart [and] throat. When prāṇa reaches the junction [of] the navel, it drives away disease [in] the navel. [So the practice] should be done regularly.

51-55.
Now the bandha of the name jālandhara is to be done at the end of inhalation. This [bandha is of] the form [of] contraction [of] the throat, obstructing the path of vāyu. When the throat is contracted by quickly bending down, the prāṇa is on the western thread in the middle on its way through brahmanāḍī. Staying in the same posture as before and stirring up saraswatī, one gradually controls the prāṇa. On the first day, four [rounds] of kumbhaka should be done, on the second [day], ten times, then five singly, [and] on the third day twenty times. Kumbhaka should always be practised together with the three bandhas [and] with an increase of five [rounds] each day.

56-58.
Disease is quickly caused by sleeping during the day, staying awake late at night, too much sexual intercourse, continual socialising, obstructions [of] urine [and] faeces, bad habit [of] irregular eating and [too much] energy through mental exertion. If the yogin stops [the practice], saying 'My disease has appeared through the practice of yoga', then he gives up his practice. This is said [to be] the first obstacle [to yoga].

59-61.
The second is called doubt, the third inattentiveness, the fourth laziness, the fifth sleep, the sixth erratic [practice], the seventh confusion, the eighth distress, the ninth lack of faith, and the tenth is called by the wise the inability to attain the essence of yoga. Thus, after reflecting [on these], the wise one should forgo these ten obstacles.

62-65.
Thus the practice of prāṇāyāma should always be performed

by meditating steadily on purity. Then the mind is dissolved in suṣumnā [and] prāṇa pervades [it]. When the impurities have withered away, and with movement up [the suṣumnā], he then becomes a yogin. Apāna moving downwards should be raised upwards by contracting it with force. This is called mūlabandha. Apāna, having been raised up, moves together with agni to the seat of prāṇa. Then agni, having united prāṇa and apāna, quickly goes to kuṇḍalinī [who is] coiled, fast asleep.

66-69a.

Thus [kuṇḍalinī], heated by agni and stirred up by vāyu, now stretches out her body inside the mouth [of] suṣumnā. Then, having pierced *brahmagranthi* produced by *rajoguṇa*, she blazes forthwith like a stroke of lightning at the mouth [of] suṣumnā. She immediately proceeds up through *viṣṇugranthi*, abiding in the heart. She goes upwards and continues through *rudragranthi,* which comes from the eyebrow centre. Then, having pierced [it], she goes to the *maṇḍala* of the moon.

69b-73.

There it dries up by itself the fluid produced by the moon in the cakra called *anāhata,* which has sixteen petals. The blood, when agitated through the force of prāṇa, [becomes] bile through contact [with] the sun, [then] having gone to the sphere [of] the moon, where it exists as the fluid nature of pure phlegm. How is [blood, which is] by nature cold, converted into heat [when] it is poured out there? In exactly the same manner, the white form of the moon is heated intensely. Because of its desire for enjoyment, the mind is externalised among sensory objects. The aspirant, enjoying this high state, rejoices in [and] abides in the self.

74-76.

Kuṇḍalinī goes to the place [where she takes] the eight forms [of] nature, and, embracing [her Lord she], attains Śiva [and] is dissolved [in him]. Thus the white matter [which] falls down, after that goes by means of the vital air to Śiva, and then prāṇa and apāna are always produced equally. It transcends whatever is small and even not small or describable. The entire prāṇa fires up like gold [heated by] the earth's fire.

77-78.
Then the body, [which is] a body composed of elements, becomes very pure in a deified form, produced by its pranic body. Released from the dormant state, it consists of pure consciousness. Thus, the pranic body, being in the nature of the self, [is] the commander of all.

79-81.
Thus one's true self [knows] this: the release from the existence of a wife, the illusion of the nature of time, as [is] the belief [that] a rope [is] like a snake. All [that] arises [is] indeed false; indeed [all that] dissolves [is] false. Just as the idea [of] silver in mother-of-pearl [is] an illusion, [so is that] of man and wife. The earth and the cosmos [are] one and the same, as [are] the soul which passes like a thread through the universe and its symbol. Sleep and the primordial spirit [are] one and the same, [as are] the light of consciousness and pure intelligence.

82-83a.
The śakti called kuṇḍalinī, luminous [and] like the lotus-fibre, seeing with the tip of her hood the bulb at the base, similar to the bulb of the lotus, [and] grasping her tail with her mouth, she connects with the brahmarandhra.

83b-87.
[When] the yogin has taken his place in padmāsana, his anus contracted, making the vāyu go upwards [and] the mind enter kumbhaka, [then] agni, through the force [of] the gust of vāyu, goes in flames to svādhiṣṭhāna. The blowing [of] the gusts of agni and vāyu through the serpent [which] then having pierced brahmagranthi, next stabs viṣṇugranthi and, after piercing rudragranthi, the six lotuses. [Now] Śakti [is]

happy [to be] with Śiva in the thousand-petalled lotus. Thus it should be understood [that] this [is] the highest state; it alone produces bliss.

**Chapter Two**

1-4a.
Now I shall describe the *vidyā* called *khecarī*, since [there is] in this place no death [or] old age [for] those who are endowed with this knowledge. Whoever is at the mercy of death, disease and old age, having learned this vidyā, o Sage, [and] having strengthened his mind, should then practise khecarī. One should respectfully approach with total devotion the guru, the destroyer [of] old age, death [and] disease on earth, who knows khecarī [and has learned] its meaning both from books and continual practice.

4b-10.
The vidyā [of] khecarī [is] difficult to attain; its practice [is] also difficult to attain. Practice and *melana* are not accomplished at the same time. Those [who are] intent on practice alone do not gain melana. One obtains the practice, o Brahman, at some time in another life, but one does not attain melana even after a hundred lives. Having performed the practice through many births [and] perfected it, a yogin attains melana at some time in a future birth. If a yogin attains melana from the mouth of the guru, then he obtains that *siddhi* spoken of in the eternal sacred teachings. If he attains melana through its meaning in books, then he reaches Śiva [and is] freed from all reincarnations. Even gurus may not be able to have this knowledge without the sacred books. Therefore, o Sage, this teaching [is] very difficult to acquire.

11-16a.
An ascetic should go wandering for as long as he does not have [this] knowledge. When he does obtain the knowledge, then the siddhi is firmly in his hand. Without this knowledge, the siddhi cannot be manifested in the three worlds.

Therefore [it is] the imperishable one [who], giving the teachings, readily gives melana. [The yogin] seeks refuge in Śiva, regarding [him as] the bestower of the practice. Having obtained this teaching from the highly honoured ones, he should not reveal [it] to others. Therefore this deep knowledge should, with every effort, be kept secret. O Brahman, having gone there where dwells a guru [who] imparts the divine yoga, and having comprehended the khecarī vidyā expressed by him, one should, undaunted right from the start, do the practice correctly as described by him. Through this knowledge, the yogin may become part of the siddhi of khecarī.

16b-18a.
Having expanded the bīja of khecarī by uniting khecarī with the energy of khecarī, he becomes Lord of the Khecaras and lives forever amongst them. Khecarī-bīja is described as the abode of the khecaras [and is] adorned [like] a circle [of] fire and water. Through this, yoga is perfected.

18b-21a.
The ninth sound [of] the phase of the moon should be pronounced in reverse. Then it is told [there is] a sound [made of] three phases [of] the form of the moon. Then also the eighth sound [pronounced] in the opposite direction [is] supreme, o Sage. Know [that] it is supreme [and] its beginning [is] the fifth, and this is said [to be] the peak of the moon in its great part. This [which gives] success in all yogas is to be gained through instruction by the guru.

21b-24a.
Whoever repeats [this] twelve [times] every day does not get even in sleep the *māya* [which is] born of the body [and] the source [of] hidden actions. And he who is self-disciplined repeats this five hundred thousand times, to him the siddhi of the glorious khecarī comes forth spontaneously. All obstructions disappear and the devas rejoice; and without doubt there will be elimination of wrinkles and grey hair.

24b-27.

Having obtained this great knowledge, one should then do the practice. Otherwise, o Brahman, one will suffer without [gaining] siddhi on the path of khecarī. Whoever does not gain this nectar-like knowledge through this cleansing practice, having gained it at the beginning of melana, should repeat it forever. If not, o Brahman, who is lacking it, does not get even a small part of siddhi. If he obtains this teaching, then he should practise its knowledge. Then the sage quickly obtains that siddhi handed down [to him].

28-37a.

Having drawn up [the tongue from] the root of the palate, the knower of ātman should for seven days clear every impurity [from it] in the way described by his guru. [He should take] a clean, oiled and sharp knife resembling the leaf of the *snuhi* plant, then with it [make a] cut the size of a hair. He should quickly apply [it] with crushed rock-salt and sea-salt. When he has completed the seventh day, he should again cut off [a piece] the size of a hair. So, having made constant effort, he should continue steadily. In six months the root of the organ of taste attached to the head is destroyed. Then the yogin who knows the right time and method should enclose with cloth the head [of] the mighty Lord of Speech, slowly elevating [it]. Again through daily friction for a period of six months, o Sage, it reaches up to the eyebrow centre and sideways up to the opening of the ears. And then, gradually set in motion, it proceeds to the root [of] the chin. Then again, after the third year, it progresses easily upwards to where the hair meets the forehead, [then] sideways up to *shakha,* the aperture at the top back of the head, o Sage, [and] downwards to the throat-pit. In another three years, having reached *brahmarandhra*, it without doubt remains there. It goes sideways to beneath the crest of hair, downwards right to the throat-pit and very slowly through the great adamantine doors of the skull.

37b-40a.

The knowledge concerning the seed sound, [which] was explained previously, is indeed extraordinary. One should do the six parts of this [vidyā] through its six different tones. One should do mystic hand movements for the purpose of [attaining] all the first siddhis. This practice should be prepared slowly [and] not all at the same time, since the body which practises [it] all at once quickly decomposes. Therefore, the practice should be done very gradually, o Esteemed Sage.

40b-44a.

Then the tongue moves to the brahmarandhra through the outer path. And then, having been rubbed with the finger-tips, the tongue enters the bolt of Brahma, [which] is difficult to be pierced even by the gods. Having done this for three years, it moves through to the entrance to Brahma. Now, having moved through to the entrance to Brahma, it performs churning perfectly. Inspired people sometimes reach the goal without churning. Whoever masters khecarī mantra may attain without churning. One obtains the fruits quickly by doing both repetition of mantra and churning.

44b-49.

Having attached a thin rod made of gold, silver or even iron to the nostrils by means of a thread impregnated with milk, holding the breath in the heart, the self [in] a comfortable position [and] focusing the eyes on the eyebrow centre, one should slowly perform the auspicious mathana. In six months the state of mathana comes naturally, just like the state of sleep in children is maintained. One should not always practise [this] excellent mathana [every] month. The yogin should not always revolve his tongue [on] the path. After twelve years there is sure [to be] attainment of siddhis. The whole universe is seen in the body [as] indistinct from the atman. This great path [of] ascending kuṇḍalīni is the infinite ruler [of] the cosmos.

**Chapter Three**

The Lotus-born said:

1-2.
O Śaṅkara, which one, the night of the dark moon or the beginning of the full moon, is described as its sign? This [is] truly [its] name. It should be established when is not the right time: the first day of the lunar fortnight, or the night of the dark moon, or the day of the full moon. This [is] the way, and no other.

3-4a.
[When there is] longing for sensual enjoyment because of desire, one is deluded by the desire for sensual enjoyment. One should renounce [these] two [and] forever devote oneself to that which is stainless. Moreover, one should abandon everything pleasurable, which one wishes for oneself.

4b-7a.
Having put *manas* within *śakti*, manas being amongst śakti, and viewed manas through manas, one leaves this highest stage. For manas [is] indeed the *bindu*, and the cause [of] creation and continued existence. Bindu comes into existence through manas, just as ghee comes from milk. Its mental cause [is] definitely not situated in the middle of bondage. Binding [is] there where śakti is located between the moon and the sun.

7b-9a.
Having known the suṣumnā [and] its piercing, moved the prāṇa up the centre, and remained in the site of the moon, one should close the nostrils. Having experienced the prāṇa, the bindu as described, the quality of *sattva* and the six cakras, one enters the sphere of joy.

9b-13.
[They are] *mūlādhāra, svādhiṣṭhāna, maṇipura* the third,

*anāhata, viśuddhi,* and *ājñā,* the sixth. It is said the base [cakra is] in the anus, svādhiṣṭhāna in the sexual [region], maṇipura in the area of the navel, anāhata is placed in the heart, viśuddhi at the base of the throat, and ājñā cakra in the skull. Having experienced the six cakras, one enters the sphere of joy. Having drawn in the vāyu, one should direct [it] upwards. He becomes part of the cosmos [who] practises this breath control. Therefore one should practise [control of] vāyu, bindu, cakras and *citta.*

14-18a.
Yogins attain the pure nectar of immortality through *samādhi* alone. Just as the fire inherent in timber does not rise up without friction, so the light of wisdom does not [appear] without the practice of yoga. The light inside a pot does not shine outside. Only when the pot is broken, does the flame of light become visible. Thus, one's body is spoken of as the vessel, while its cause [is] light. When it is completely broken by the speech of the guru, the divine wisdom of Brahma becomes clear. Having attained [it and] made the guru the helmsman, one crosses the subtle dimension and the ocean of worldly existence through the power [of] the desire for sādhana.

18b-21a.
That aforesaid [*vāc*], [which] sprouts in *para*, makes two leaves in *paśyanti,* buds in *madhyama* [and] blossoms in *vaikhari*, becomes set by reversing this order. The supreme divinity is at the peak of *vāc.* Whoever remains always convinced that '*I am Soham'*, causes the *vāc* to blossom [and] is not even affected by various vile words [that] are spoken.

21b-26.
The three [states of consciousness]: waking, dreaming and deep sleep; and the three [aspects of existence]: the entire manifest universe, the cosmic subtle body and the supreme consciousness; the macrocosm and even the microcosm, the worlds of the earth and others, [all these], through absorption

in their true attributes, are merged into the inner self. The egg, heated by the fire of knowledge, is absorbed with its cause into the supreme self [and] becomes merged in the supreme Brahma. Then, still and deep, [it is neither] light nor darkness, neither describable nor distinct. Reflect on the ātman resting within the body, like a light inside a jar. Just the essence remains. One should think of the ātman [as] the size of a thumb, a form of light, without smoke, shining within, unchangeable and imperishable.

27-29.
The *vijñāna ātman* in the body is deluded by the unreal [during the states of] waking, dreaming and sleeping. At last, after many births, as a result of good karma, it wishes to return to its true state. Who am I? How did this disease called *samsāra* come to [me]? What happens during deep sleep to me, who is active in mundane life in [the states of] waking and dreaming? It asks, having become engrossed in reflection through its own light, above all.

30-32.
The reflected consciousness, because of its lack of wisdom, is burned by an external heat, just like a bale of cotton is burnt by fire. When *jñāna* has been destroyed, the inner self located in the ether immediately [expresses] the highest *vijñāna*, permeating everything, [and] having maintained both *manomaya* and *jñānamaya*, now burns [them] one by one. Then it shines forth from within, like a clear light inside a pot.

33-35.
The muni, who remains meditating right until sleep and death, is to be known as a *jīvanmukta* [who], having done his duty, [is] blessed. Renouncing the state of jīvanmukta, when in time his body has decomposed, [he attains] liberation from the body, its breath unmoving. Only that remains which [is] imperishable, without sound, touch or form, that is, the

essence, eternal and odourless, without beginning or end, beyond great, permanent, pure [and] untainted.

Thus [ends] the Upaniṣad.

# ABOUT THE AUTHOR

Swami Satyadharma is a senior sannyasin, a yoga acharya, and a versatile teacher of yogic meditation and allied philosophies, having a Master of Arts in Yoga Philosophy with First Class Honors from Bihar Yoga Bharati, India. She wrote the commentary on the *Yoga Chudamani Upanishad*, while living in India, which was published by Yoga Publications Trust in 2003. In 2015 she published her commentary on *Yoga Tattwa Upanishad,* and in 2018 her commentary on *Yoga Darshan Upanishad.*

Born in Connecticut USA, she lived in India for over 35 years under the direct tutelage of her yoga master, Swami Satyananda Saraswati, where she imbibed the traditional yogic teachings, and became Director of the Department of Undergraduate Studies at Bihar Yoga Bharati. She has compiled and edited many major yoga publications, such as *Yoga Darshan, Sannyasa Darshan, Dharana Darshan* and the *Teachings of Swami Satyananda.* Now based in Australia, she lives a life of sadhana and introspection, while continuing to elucidate the ancient teachings of yoga in the form of the twenty Yoga Upanishads.

# ABOUT THE TRANSLATOR

Srimukti (Ruth Perini) was for many years a teacher of yoga and meditation. Already a linguist, having graduated in French, Italian and Japanese from the Universities of Sydney and Queensland, Australia, she undertook four years of studies in Sanskrit at the Australian National University (ANU) with Dr McComas Taylor. She was invited to join the Golden Key International Society for outstanding academic achievement, as she was awarded High Distinctions throughout her Sanskrit studies. She is the translator of *Yoga Tattwa Upaniṣad* and *Yoga Darshana Upanishad*, commentaries by Swami Satyadharma. She has also translated the *Nāda Bindu* and *Dhyānabindu Upanishads*, and is currently working on the *Varāha Upaniṣad.*

Ruth (Srimukti) may be contacted on yoga.upanishads@yahoo.com.

www.ingramcontent.com/pod-product-compliance
Lightning Source LLC
Chambersburg PA
CBHW070253010526
44107CB00056B/2445
* 9 7 8 0 6 4 8 9 1 0 7 2 5 *